Stereotypes and Language Learning Motivation

This book explores stereotypes that learners of six Asian languages – Japanese, Mandarin, Korean, Myanmar, Thai and Vietnamese – hold about the target language country, its cultures and people.

Some of the findings, such as the language learners' mental images of Myanmar, Thailand and Vietnam, are presented here for the first time. Recognizing that stereotypes, and attitudes embedded in them, have an impact on people's actions and behavioural intentions, this book examines whether and how the country stereotypes held by the students influenced their motivation to learn the target language. Besides providing worthwhile insights into the content and structure of the country stereotypes and their relationship with language learning motivation, this book offers methodological and theoretical advancements. Drawing on the intellectual heritage of Russian psychologist Lev Vygotsky (1896–1934), the book highlights how the concepts of word meaning (*znachenie slova*) and word sense (*smysl*) could be fruitfully employed in studies on stereotypes that people learning a foreign language hold about a target language country.

This book will appeal to all readers interested in stereotypes that people have about foreign countries and also to educators and researchers who study language learning motivation.

Larisa Nikitina, PhD, is Senior Lecturer at the Faculty of Languages and Linguistics, University of Malaya, Malaysia. Her research interests include the psychological aspects involved in learning an additional language, approaches to the teaching of culture in the language classroom and quantitative methodologies in applied linguistics. She has published extensively on these topics.

Stereotypes and Language Learning Motivation
A Study of L2 Learners of Asian Languages

Larisa Nikitina

LONDON AND NEW YORK

First published 2020
by Routledge
2 Park Square, Milton Park, Abingdon, Oxon OX14 4RN

and by Routledge
52 Vanderbilt Avenue, New York, NY 10017

Routledge is an imprint of the Taylor & Francis Group, an informa business

© 2020 Larisa Nikitina

The right of Larisa Nikitina to be identified as author of this work has been asserted by her in accordance with sections 77 and 78 of the Copyright, Designs and Patents Act 1988.

All rights reserved. No part of this book may be reprinted or reproduced or utilised in any form or by any electronic, mechanical, or other means, now known or hereafter invented, including photocopying and recording, or in any information storage or retrieval system, without permission in writing from the publishers.

Trademark notice: Product or corporate names may be trademarks or registered trademarks, and are used only for identification and explanation without intent to infringe.

British Library Cataloguing-in-Publication Data
A catalogue record for this book is available from the British Library

Library of Congress Cataloging-in-Publication Data
A catalog record for this book has been requested

ISBN: 978-0-367-35806-8 (hbk)
ISBN: 978-0-429-34187-8 (ebk)

Typeset in Times New Roman
by Apex CoVantage, LLC

To my mother, my father and my mother-in-law

Contents

List of figures   xi
List of tables   xii
List of abbreviations   xiii

Introduction   1

Stereotypes: a ubiquitous construct 1
Structure of the book 2
References 3

1 **Stereotypes as a research focus**   4

    Stereotypes: the origins of the construct 4
    Stereotypes as an interdisciplinary construct 5
    Issues in research on stereotypes 6
       Definitions and approaches 6
       Stereotype content: country and national
          stereotypes 8
       Stereotype formation: internal and external
          processes 9
       Stereotype accuracy 11
       Individual and consensual stereotypes 13
    An overview of methodological approaches in research
       on stereotypes 14
       Exploring stereotype content: structured and
          unstructured approaches 15
          Structured approaches: check-lists and percentage
             estimates 15

       Unstructured approaches: the free-response technique 16
          Measuring stereotypes: criteria for consensus 17
          Assessing stereotype valence and salience 17
       Research on country stereotypes in applied linguistics 19
          Research focus, aims, methodologies and gaps in studies on stereotypes held by language learners 19
       References 22

2 Motivation, attitudes and stereotypes in L2 research: connecting the dots   26

       Motivation in applied linguistics research: an overview of literature 26
          Goal setting in language learning: instrumental and integrative orientations 28
       The construct of attitude in psychology and applied linguistics 31
          Attitude: etymology and definitions 31
          Research on attitudes in the field of applied linguistics 32
       Stereotypes, attitudes and L2 motivation: connecting the dots 33
          How applied linguistics research can contribute to the scholarship on stereotypes 34
       References 36

3 A mixed-methods approach to link country stereotypes and L2 motivation   40

       The aim of the study, its research questions and research design 40
       The need for mixed-methods approaches in research on country stereotypes, language attitudes and L2 motivation 42
       The research instrument 43
          The open-ended question 43
          The closed-ended items to measure L2 motivation 43
       Sampling method and the participants 44
       Data collection and organization 45
       Analysis of the qualitative data 45

The content analysis 45
　　　The coding process 47
　　　The assessments of stereotype salience and accuracy 48
　Analysis of the quantitative data 48
　　　The calculation of mean valence (MV) 49
　　　The calculation of composite mean valence (CompMV) 49
　　　The statistical analysis 50
　　　The analysis of L2 motivation: exploratory factor
　　　　analysis (EFA) 51
　　　The reliability analysis: Cronbach's alpha 51
　　　The correlation analysis: Spearman correlation test 52
　　　The regression analysis 52
　References 53

**4 Findings on language learners' country stereotypes
　and their relationships with L2 motivation** 　　　　　　　　55

　*Language learners' mental images of the target language
　　countries 55*
　　Language learners' mental images of China 55
　　　Consensual stereotypes of China 55
　　　Categories of images of China 56
　　Language learners' mental images of Japan 59
　　　Consensual stereotypes of Japan 60
　　　Categories of images of Japan 60
　　Language learners' mental images of Korea 64
　　　Consensual stereotypes of Korea 64
　　　Categories of images of Korea 66
　　Language learners' mental images of Myanmar 69
　　　Consensual stereotypes of Myanmar 70
　　　Categories of images of Myanmar 70
　　Language learners' mental images of Thailand 73
　　　Consensual stereotypes of Thailand 73
　　　Categories of images of Thailand 74
　　Language learners' mental images of Vietnam 76
　　　Consensual stereotypes of Vietnam 76
　　　Categories of images of Vietnam 77
　　A discussion of the findings on the language learners'
　　　mental images of the target language countries 79

x Contents

> Findings from the analysis of the stereotype content 79
> Finding on the attitudes embedded in the mental images of the target language countries 83
> Findings from the statistical analysis: relationships between the country stereotypes and L2 motivation 84
> Dimensions of the students' L2 motivation: results from the exploratory factor analysis (EFA) 84
> Findings from the correlation analysis 84
> Findings from the regression analysis 86
> References 86

5 **Wider implications and conclusions** 88

> *Summary of the main findings* 88
> *Methodological, theoretical and pedagogical implications* 89
> Directions for future research and practice 91
> *Conclusions* 93
> *References* 93

Appendix 1 Questionnaire on country images and L2 motivation 95
Appendix 2 Findings on language learners' country stereotypes 98
Appendix 3 SPSS codes for the regression analysis 110
Glossary 116
Index 118

Figures

3.1 Strands and steps in the research design 41
3.2 Sequence of the quantitative analysis 50

Tables

4.1	Summary of the findings on the language learners' mental images of the target language countries	80
4.2	Categories of country images and absent country-related aspects	81
A4.1	Consensual stereotypes of China	98
A4.2	Categories of images of China	99
A4.3	Consensual stereotypes of Japan	100
A4.4	Categories of images of Japan	101
A4.5	Consensual stereotypes of Korea	101
A4.6	Categories of images of Korea	102
A4.7	Consensual stereotypes of Myanmar	103
A4.8	Categories of images of Myanmar	104
A4.9	Consensual stereotypes of Thailand	105
A4.10	Categories of images of Thailand	106
A4.11	Consensual stereotypes of Vietnam	106
A4.12	Categories of images of Vietnam	107
A4.13	Findings from the EFA	107
A4.14	Findings from the Spearman rank correlation test on the relationships between the language learners' country images and L2 motivation (data aggregated for all six countries)	108
A4.15	Findings from the Spearman rank correlation test on the relationships between the language learners' country images and L2 motivation (data for each target language country)	109
A4.16	Findings from the robust multiple regression analysis	109

Abbreviations

CompMV	composite means valence
EFA	exploratory factor analysis
MV	mean valence
MVR	mean valence rank
n	number of mental images in a group of images
N	total number of mental images of a target language country
p	p-value or the probability value
r_s	Spearman's rank correlation coefficient
SI	salience index
SR	salience rank

Introduction

Stereotypes: a ubiquitous construct

Stereotypes are ubiquitous. They are also indispensable. Walter Lippmann (1889–1974), who introduced the concept of stereotypes as an object of research in the social sciences and humanities disciplines, has famously described stereotypes as "pictures in our heads". He also raised awareness that these mental images or "pictures" have the power to influence the way we see and perceive the world around us. Lippmann recognized that stereotypes serve as an indispensable cognitive device to aid the processing of an incessant flow of information that we receive in our daily life. Importantly, he acknowledged that stereotypes are not attitude-neutral: the feelings embedded in them serve as a point of reference that guides people's judgments, shapes their intentions and even determines their actions.

Stereotypes or mental images that individual people hold about various phenomena, objects, social groups, cultures and countries are formed since early childhood and via numerous channels, including the family, school, the mass media, social networks, peers and friends. As Lippmann (1922/1965) observed, "We are told about the world before we see it. We imagine most things before we experience them" (p. 59). In everyday language, the word "stereotypes" often has a negative connotation. However, stereotypes are not necessarily negative. Neither are they erroneous by default. The biggest problem with the stereotypes that we hold is that they are rigid and inflexible. Being resistant to change, stereotypes are accountable for persistent biases in our perceptions of the world around us. More importantly, the negative stereotypes that people hold about other social groups, cultures, countries and nations interfere with the full recognition of our shared "common humanity" (Lippmann, 1922/1965, p. 58). The latter point is especially pertinent in the context of foreign language education because a successful outcome of a foreign language program would entail not only a good knowledge of an additional language but also a better understanding of the

2 *Introduction*

target language country, its cultures and people. Language educators have a role to play in developing their students' more nuanced and sophisticated understanding of the world around us.

This book is an outcome of my long-standing interest in stereotypes, "pictures in the head" or mental images that learners of foreign languages bring into the language classroom. Previous studies mostly have been done among learners of various European languages, and they yielded valuable insights into the language learners' mental imagery of the target language countries. In recent years, some research studies have begun examining links between language learners' country stereotypes and their language learning motivation (L2 motivation) (Heinzmann, 2013; Nikitina, 2019). The current book pursues this line of inquiry. Its main aim is to examine relationships between country stereotypes and L2 motivation by employing a systematic and rigorous methodology that would allow connecting the dots and establishing seamless links between these two psychological constructs.

In view that a vast body of research literature is available on stereotypes that learners of European language bring into the foreign language classroom, this book explores stereotypes or mental images that learners of Asian languages hold about the target language countries and how these images influence the students' L2 motivation. The methodological rigour and the focus on learners of non-European languages make this book a first-of-its-kind inquiry into stereotypes and L2 motivation in a context of foreign language teaching and learning. Considerable attention in the book is given to the research methodology. Also, the book proposes that a theoretical framework rooted in the Vygotskian concepts of word meaning (*znachenie slova*) and word sense (*smysl*) could be a suitable foundation for research on stereotypes in the field of applied linguistics. A more detailed overview of the book's structure is given in the following section.

Structure of the book

Subsequent to this Introduction, Chapter 1 presents the construct of stereotypes as a focus of research. It reviews relevant studies on stereotypes, especially country and national stereotypes, in various academic disciplines and highlights some methodological issues faced by researchers. Chapter 2 offers a review of literature on this book's other key constructs – attitudes and language learning motivation (L2 motivation). It argues that applied linguistics, being a discipline at the confluence of several academic fields, is well positioned to connect the dots and establish theoretical and empirical links between endogenous stereotypes of target language countries held by language learners, the students' language attitudes and their L2 motivation. The chapter proposes the Vygotskian concepts of word meaning *znachenie slova* and word sense (*smysl*) as an overarching theoretical foundation for such studies. Chapter 2 sets the stage for a rigorous and comprehensive analysis offered in this book.

Chapter 3 explains the methodology adopted for the analysis of stereotypes, language attitudes and L2 motivation. The chapter provides a detailed description of the qualitative and quantitative strands of the analytical procedure. It highlights the importance of employing mixed-methods research designs in studies on language learners' mental images of target language countries, their cultures and people. Chapter 4 presents the findings. Firstly, it describes consensual stereotypes of the six Asian target language countries and reports their favourability and salience parameters. Then it discusses the content of larger categories of images of each country. Some tentative propositions are put forward in the chapter regarding the relationships between the country stereotypes and students' L2 motivation. Secondly, the chapter presents results of statistical analyses that shed light on the nature of these relationships. To wrap up the discussion, the chapter summarizes and synthesizes the findings from the qualitative and quantitative strands of the analytical procedure. The concluding chapter, Chapter 5, presents wider implications that can be drawn from this study and its findings.

It is much hoped that this scholarly endeavour will contribute to the existing knowledge about stereotypes and country images that learners of foreign languages bring into the language classroom, and that it will enhance our understanding of the relationships between these stereotypes and language learning motivation. It is also my hope that the methods, theories and approaches presented in this book will be useful for other researchers in their future explorations of "pictures in the heads" that people have of the surrounding world.

Last but not least, I would like to acknowledge my intellectual debt to Professor Dr Urmas Sutrop, from whom I have learned about salience measurement methodologies, which have allowed much more rigorous explorations of language learners' stereotypes, and which have made such explorations so much more exciting.

References

Heinzmann, S. (2013). *Young language learners' motivation and attitudes: Longitudinal, comparative and explanatory perspectives*. New York, NY: Bloomsbury.

Lippmann, W. (1922/1965). *Public opinion*. New York, NY: The Free Press.

Nikitina, L. (2019). Do country stereotypes influence language learning motivation? A study among foreign language learners in Malaysia. *Moderna Språk, 113*(1), 58–79.

1 Stereotypes as a research focus

Stereotypes: the origins of the construct

The word "stereotype" is derived from the Ancient Greek words *stereós* ("solid") and *typos* ("mark, impression, type"). Its original meaning in the English language referred to a solid metal plate used for printing. The etymology and usage of the term "stereotype" highlight the connotations to rigidity, permanence, repetition and inflexibility. British author James Morier (1780–1849) was the first person to use the word "stereotype" as a reference to perceptions and traditions rooted in a culture (Rudmin, 1989). Over time, the word "stereotype" acquired a figurative meaning of "something continued or constantly repeated without change" (*Oxford English Dictionary*, 1991, p. 651).

Walter Lippmann devoted a whole chapter in his influential book, *Public Opinion* (1922/1965), to people's stereotypical perceptions of the surrounding world. As he persuasively demonstrated, such stereotypes are not limited to the perceptions of other people, social, cultural, ethnic or gender groups. Stereotypes also encompass "symbolic pictures" of foreign countries (p. 8). Writing in the year 1922, Lippmann gave examples of contemporary perceptions of Britain as "the Defender of Public Law" and of "America the Crusader" (p. 8). It should be noted that Lippmann (1922/1965) did not provide a scientific definition of stereotypes but instead described them metaphorically as "pictures in our heads" through which we view "the world outside" (p. 3). However, he raised and addressed several important issues related to the construct of stereotypes, including the sources and functions of stereotypes, their maintenance and perpetuation as well as cultural and affective aspects involved in stereotyping.

Lippmann (1922/1965) recognized that stereotypes are rooted in and originate within a culture. As he stated, "we pick out what our culture has already defined for us" (p. 55). He argued that stereotypes serve as an important cognitive device that helps people to effectively deal with a constant inflow of new information. Describing the utility of stereotypes as a cognitive shortcut, Lippmann noted that there is an "economy" in stereotyping (p. 59). To support this proposition, he argued that people would not resort to stereotypes when they deal with familiar phenomena. In other words, "In a circle of friends, and in relation to close associates or competitors, there is no shortcut through, and no substitute for, an individualized understanding" (Lippmann, 1922/1965, p. 59).

Importantly, Lippmann's book raised awareness of the inseparability of stereotypes from culture, which elucidates the tenacious and pervading nature of stereotypes. To explain how stereotypes are maintained and perpetuated he posited that stereotypes are handed down as a form of cultural knowledge or cultural heritage from one generation to another by "parents, teachers, priests, and uncles" (Lippmann, 1922/1965, p. 61). Because of this, people accumulate ideas about various phenomena before they have had a chance to explore the world for themselves and before they can form their own ideas about them. A notable argument put forward by Lippmann is that stereotypes as a product of a culture are also "the fortress of our tradition" upon which individual people hinge their judgment of the surrounding world. Because of this, "A pattern of stereotypes is not neutral. . . . The stereotypes are . . . highly charged with the feelings that are attached to them" (p. 64). In other words, stereotypes are evaluative in nature. Another important observation made by Lippmann was that stereotypes are not necessarily false or wrong. After all, they do serve as an important cognitive device. However, when the tendency of the human mind to generalize about the nature of things and events supplants its ability to note "the ebb and flow of affairs" (p. 73), then stereotypes become accountable for the biases and errors in our thinking.

Stereotypes as an interdisciplinary construct

Stereotypes are an interdisciplinary construct. They have been researched and discussed in various academic fields. Summarizing developments in research on national and country stereotypes in the 20th century, Clark (1990) noted that studies on stereotypes were initiated in the academic field of cultural anthropology. In the 1930s, the interest in this topic intensified due to the publication of Ruth Benedict's book *Patterns of Culture* (1934). In the second and third decades of the 20th century, social psychologists produced several influential studies on national and country stereotypes. As Clark (1990) observed, the interest in research on national and country stereotypes intensified during World War II (1939–1945) when the US government was sponsoring big research projects on national character because of these studies' political and ideological importance. The insights obtained from such studies were used to develop effective strategies for psychological warfare. Also, a better understanding of national character helped to ease occasional tensions between the World War II Allies.

In the post-war years, the interest in national stereotypes began to wane among cultural anthropologists. However, since the 1940s, the topic has been actively researched in other academic fields, including political science, intercultural relations, media studies, tourism studies, social psychology, literature studies and applied linguistics (Nikitina, 2017b). The greatest share of this research has been conducted by psychology researchers (Schneider, 2005). The avid interest of the scientific community in stereotypes is due to the important practical implications that stem from garnering deeper insights into the mechanisms involved in stereotyping. For example, researchers have established that there exist links between stereotypes and prejudice. An influential study by Allport (1954) demonstrated how the stereotypes held by people can influence their actions and behavioural intentions, including discriminatory behaviour, toward members of other ethnic and social groups.

The interdisciplinary nature of stereotypes, a perspective this book adopts, allows for a cross-pollination of ideas among academic disciplines. It also enables us to draw on a variety of intellectual resources to solve methodological and theoretical issues faced by the researchers. The following section highlights the main issues of research on stereotypes.

Issues in research on stereotypes

Definitions and approaches

It is important to examine how stereotypes have been defined. As Schneider (2005) noted, "definitions are not epistemologically neutral; they divide the world the way someone wants it to be divided" (p. 15). In other words, the definition proposed by a researcher would highlight the attributes that are essential to his or her conceptualization of the construct and, by necessity, the definition would obfuscate properties that are deemed by the researcher to be less relevant. In their influential study of national stereotypes, Katz and Braly (1933) defined this construct as "a fixed impression which conforms very little to the facts it pretends to represent and results from our defining first and observing second" (p. 181). This definition echoes Lippmann's discussion of stereotypes: it highlights their inflexible nature and acknowledges the presence of cognitive processes involved in stereotyping (i.e., "defining first and observing second"). Since the pioneering research by Katz and Braly, stereotypes have been defined "in myriad ways" (Spencer-Rodgers, 2001, p. 641). For the most part, studies in psychology operationalized stereotypes as perceptions of and generalizations about other people and social groups. This marked a shift from Lippmann's (1922/1965) view of stereotypes as individually held mental pictures of the world at large. This narrowing of the domain is well justified because social psychology deals with stereotyping in the context of the person-to-person or group-to-group interactions, perceptions and evaluations.

An analysis done by Schneider (2005, pp. 16–17) of definitions of stereotypes in research literature revealed that stereotypes are often defined as "mental representations" (see Stangor and Lange, 1994, p. 359) or as a set of beliefs about traits and characteristics of other persons or groups of individuals (see Ashmore and Del Boca, 1979; Harding, Proshansky, Kutner and Chein, 1969; Jones, 1997; Mackie, 1973; Oskamp and Schultz, 2005; Stephan, 1985). Some researchers included in their definitions aspects pertaining to stereotype accuracy, and they proposed that stereotypes may be true or false (Harding et al., 1969). One school of thought in psychology research places emphasis on the shared or collective nature of stereotypes (Harding et al., 1969; Jones, 1997; Mackie, 1973). An alternative view is that the definition of stereotypes needs not be constrained by the presence of consensual agreement (Hamilton, Stroessner and Driscoll, 1994). Generally, psychologists agree that stereotypes can be either positive or negative (Jones, 1997, p. 170).

As this brief overview shows, there is no standardized set of features that are attached to the construct of stereotypes in all or even the majority of the definitions. Among the existing operationalizations, the definition that is theoretically and epistemologically closest to the current study was proposed by Jones (1997) who considered stereotypes as:

> a positive or negative set of beliefs held by an individual about the characteristics of a group of people. It varies in its accuracy, the extent to which it captures the degree to which the stereotyped group members possess these traits, and the extent to which the set of beliefs is shared by others.
>
> (p. 179)

Though this definition is restricted to stereotypes about social groups, it includes several pertinent to the present study aspects, namely, the evaluative nature of stereotypes and the degree of consensus to distinguish a stereotype. In this book, a stereotype is defined as a mental image about a target language country, its cultures and people held by language learners. The terms "stereotypes", "stereotypical images", "country stereotypes" and "mental images" are used interchangeably.

Stereotype content: country and national stereotypes

In social psychology research, stereotype content or what a stereotype consists of refers to "specific attributes that are believed to characterize a group of people" (Spencer-Rodgers, 2001, p. 642). These attributes can include perceived typical behaviours as well as physical, personality and demographic characteristics of a group of people or distinct individuals. From a broader perspective, stereotype content may include mental images of any object – and not necessarily a social group – as well as beliefs about traits and characteristics of this object (Lippmann, 1922/1965). Notably, Messick and Mackie (1989) proposed that not only mental images but also "attitudes and feelings" (p. 50) can form stereotype content. For example, stereotype content about a foreign country may include mental representations of this country, beliefs about its geography, climate, political system, history, culture, language, specific sites, events and local people; it also can incorporate the moods, feelings and affective reactions (e.g., "happy", "romantic", "beautiful") that people associate with this particular country (Brijs, Bloemer and Kasper, 2011; Echtner and Ritchie, 1993).

Substantial research literature is available on country stereotypes, national character and national stereotypes. To distinguish among these terms, "national character" refers to "the shared perception of personality characteristics typical of citizens of a particular nation" (McCrae and Terracciano, 2006, p. 156). In a similar way, "national stereotypes" are "the distinctive characteristics about other nations that spontaneously spring to mind" (McCrae and Terracciano, 2006, p. 156). A broader term, "country stereotypes", includes not only the beliefs about a country's inhabitants, but it also incorporates mental images of a country itself and of various phenomena to be found in this country (Brijs et al., 2011; Herz and Diamantopoulos, 2013). Research studies in applied linguistics do not draw a sharp distinction between the three terms; they usually explore these three aspects under the umbrella of country stereotypes (see Nikitina, 2017b). In line with this tendency, the current book does not draw a sharp distinction between country stereotypes, national character and national stereotypes. It focuses on stereotypes or mental images that language learners hold about target language countries and recognizes that these stereotypes may include references to characteristics of the target language country *per se* (e.g., its geography and climate), descriptions of people who live in this country (e.g., their perceived character and physical appearance) and perceptions of the target culture. The analysis of stereotype content in this book also considers what is lacking in the student's images of the target language countries.

Stereotype formation: internal and external processes

A prominent area in psychology research on stereotypes is the processes involved in stereotype formation. These studies approach the issue either by exploring the internal cognitive processes associated with stereotyping or by focusing on the external social forces that shape these stereotypes. Among the former, especially pertinent for the current book, are the studies that examine how national stereotypes are formed in the minds of young children. As to the latter, particularly illuminating would be scholarly explorations that focus on the influence of social sources on the content of national stereotypes.

Earlier studies on the formation of national stereotypes in children's minds have given ample empirical evidence indicating that stereotypes about other nations and countries are culturally rooted and imbibed since early childhood. A large-scale study by Lambert and Klineberg (1967) among 3300 children in 11 countries discovered that the first national stereotype formed in the mind of a child is the stereotype about his or her own national group. Studies among children aged between 4 and 15 years old in various geographical and cultural contexts support this proposition, and researchers have persuasively demonstrated that by the age of 10, children attain full awareness of their own national group (Enesco, Navarro, Paradela and Guerrero, 2005; Piaget and Weil, 1951). For example, Piaget and Weil (1951), who conducted research among 200 children in Switzerland, found out that by the age of 10, "the notion of country becomes a reality and takes on the idea of homeland in the child's mind" (p. 565).

Regarding the internal mechanisms of national and country stereotype formation, researchers recognize that both cognitive and affective undercurrents are involved in this process. As Piaget and Weil (1951) put it, "The child's gradual realization that he belongs to a particular country presupposes a parallel process of cognitive and affective development" (p. 563). At the cognitive level, categorization, which involves assigning differences and making comparisons between the child's own and other national groups, plays an important role. Interestingly, children tend to view their own national group in a much more positive light in comparison to their perceptions of other nations. Piaget and Weil (1951) discovered that Swiss children in their study possessed predominantly negative stereotypes about "foreigners". Some of the children's statements cited by the researchers were "the French are poor and everything's dirty there", "the Germans are bad, they're always making war", "the Americans are stupid" and the Russians are "bad, they're always wanting to make war" (pp. 569–570). When asked about the sources of their knowledge and opinions about other nations, it became clear that the children had absorbed them from the surrounding social environment.

As the children explained, "Everyone says so", "I've heard it ... that's what people say" and "I've heard people say so and you hear it on the wireless, and at school" (Piaget and Weil, 1951, pp. 569–571). These findings empirically support a proposition made by Lippmann (1922/1965) as early as the 1920s that external factors, such as the cultural context, play a crucial role in the internal processes of stereotype formation.

To concur, Bar-Tal (1997) pointed out that "stereotypic content is not universal, but is culturally and individually bound" (p. 492). He maintained that narrations about past relations are important because "past wars, animosity, hostility or, in contrast, help, cooperation and friendship have a cumulative impact over time on the present nature of intergroup relations, reflected also in the contents of group members' stereotypes" (p. 496). The mass media and popular culture play an important part in the weaving of such narratives, and they have been identified among the most powerful external sources that influence the formation of stereotypes about countries and nations (Smith, 1973). The influences from these external sources cannot be overestimated, especially in the contexts where direct contacts between an individual person's own culture and target culture are lacking or non-existent. In such situations, the only available sources of information about unfamiliar cultures are the representations that are ubiquitous in the mass media or on the internet, that are ever present in popular discourses, in popular novels and motion pictures. In the context of foreign language education, Steele and Suozzo (as cited in Allen, 2004, p. 235) noted that language learners' stereotypes about the target language countries are "the products of their own enculturation and media bombardment".

It has been highlighted in research literature that the mass media and Hollywood-made movies often promote distorted images of certain cultures, countries and their inhabitants. De Luca Braun (2003), who conducted a study on the portrayal of Italian people in Hollywood movies, found that the movies tended to show Italians, including Italian Americans, predominantly in a negative light. As she pointed out, "of the more than 1,000 Hollywood films featuring Italian or Italian American characters made between 1928 and 2000, nearly three-quarters portray them as gangsters, boors, buffoons, bigots or bimbos" (De Luca Braun, 2003, p. 4). In a similar vein, Shaheen's (2003) study revealed that out of 900 sampled Hollywood movies only 5 percent depict Arabs as "normal, human characters" (p. 171). It should be noted that a lack of understanding of the inherent complexity and polymorphism of the target culture can be found in the foreign language textbooks as well. For example, Skubikowski (1985) discovered that some Italian language textbooks promoted popular stereotypes and cultural clichés about Italy.

Stereotypes as a research focus 11

The present book does not aim to explore mechanisms involved in the formation and maintenance of country stereotypes. However, the concept of a system of meaning developed by Russian psychologist Lev Vygotsky (1896–1934) could offer a suitable foundation for explorations of how external and internal mechanisms intertwine in, and contribute to, the formation of stereotypes. The book also recognizes that foreign language educators play a mediating role in these processes. Language teachers are instrumental in making the students re-evaluate, deconstruct and, most importantly, become aware of the rigid reductionist perceptions that people tend to have about other countries and cultures. Employing a Vygotskian concept of a system of meaning, Chapter 5 discusses some implications that research on country stereotypes has for pedagogical practice.

Stereotype accuracy

Stereotype accuracy is one of the central and most debated issues in psychology research. Some researchers view stereotypes as *a priori* false notions, which is reflected in their definitions of the construct (e.g., Katz and Braly, 1933, 1935). Furthermore, stereotypes about national character have been regarded as not only lacking in accuracy but also as pure "fiction" (McCrae and Terracciano, 2006, p. 160; Robins, 2005; Terracciano et al., 2005). Arguing why stereotypes cannot be accurate, Robins (2005) pointed out that "stereotypes about national characters seem to be social constructions designed to serve specific societal purposes" (p. 63). As such, they tend to vary from one socio-cultural context to another and across historical and political epochs. Similar views are espoused by researchers in the social sciences and humanities. For example, Bar-Tal (1997) observed that people receive the "facts" that form their stereotypes about other nations through various transmitting mechanisms where these facts undergo a selective process.

Another dilemma faced by researchers is whether stereotypes should be approached from an emic or an etic perspective. When viewing national stereotypes from an etic perspective, a researcher would inevitably face the problem of "so many people, so many opinions". As Boulding (1959) noted, "A nation is some complex of the images of the persons who contemplate it, and as there are many different persons, so there are many different images" (p. 121). This could be one of the reasons as to why stereotypes about the same national group are often contradictory. As Leerssen (2003) aptly put it:

> Countries are always contradictory in a specific way: their most characteristic attribute always involves its own opposite. Thus Frenchmen are either formal, rational, cool, distanced (type: Giscard d'Estaing) or else

excitable, sanguine, passionate (type: Louis de Funès); the English are either tea-drinking, respectable and with a "stiff upper lip" (type: Miss Marple or Phileas Fogg) or else robust, no-nonsense, nonconformist and easily offended (type: Winston Churchill, John Bull); the Dutch are either fearless defenders of tolerance and liberty, or else boring bourgeois obsessed with cleaning windows, etc., etc.

(para. 14)

Some researchers have observed that stereotypes that people hold about other cultures, especially about the neighbouring national groups, tend to be the opposite from the images that people have of their own nation (Realo et al., 2009). The other national groups are often assigned negative qualities which are considered as non-existent or negligible in one's own group. For example, in a study by Lindsay (1997), the Scottish participants provided overwhelmingly positive stereotypes of their own national group which they considered as "friendly", "warm", "political" and "unpretentious". At the same time, they viewed their neighbours in England as "arrogant", "aloof" and "opinionated" (p. 8). This tendency of viewing "the other", especially neighbouring or competing groups, in a predominantly negative light presents a strong argument against stereotypes as accurate reflections of reality. Clearly, attempts to achieve a definitive conclusion regarding the veracity of *national* stereotypes could well be abandoned.

In contrast, it could be possible to gauge the accuracy of *country* stereotypes with a good degree of certainty. Nikitina and Furuoka (2013c) proposed that the "common–unique" continuum developed by Echtner and Ritchie (1993) might be employed as a heuristic device to assess the accuracy of language learners' stereotypes of target language countries. To be more specific, at the "common" end of the continuum would be placed the country images that refer to general features or give vague descriptors of a target language country (e.g., "cold climate" or "located in Asia"). In contrast, the images placed at the "unique" point of the continuum would refer to specific sites and particular phenomena that can be found in that particular country (e.g., "the city of Stockholm" as an image of Sweden, or "the Bon Odori festival" as a stereotype of Japan). Using this heuristic approach, the veracity of the images at the "unique" end of the continuum would give empirical evidence regarding the accuracy of the country stereotypes held by language learners. Conclusions regarding stereotype accuracy in this study were reached using heuristic properties of the "common–unique" continuum (see Chapter 4). However, this book recognizes that a high accuracy of stereotypes is not equal to a deep understanding of a target language country.

Notwithstanding the on-going debate concerning the accuracy of national and country stereotypes, researchers working in various academic disciplines (e.g., Leerssen, 2003 in literary studies; Lindsay, 1997 in political science; McCrae and Terracciano, 2006 in social psychology) agree that with regard to national and country stereotypes, the matter of importance is not whether these stereotypes are true or false. What really matters is whether people are consciously aware of a human tendency to use cognitive shortcuts and to rely on a set of pre-existing inflexible stereotypes when processing the constant inflow of information, and whether they are cognizant of the influence that these stereotypes exercise over our attitudes and behaviours toward "the other". This concern is shared by language educators. In their study of country stereotypes held by German language learners, Schulz and Haerle (1995) aptly noted that while these stereotypes "can be true, party true, or patently false" (p. 34), the role of language educators is to develop in their students a critical awareness that, if left unchecked, these stereotypes will hamper productive cross-cultural communication and understanding.

Individual and consensual stereotypes

Lippmann (1922/1965) considered stereotypes as "pictures in the heads" of individual people and also as mutually shared beliefs among a group of people. Social psychologists acknowledge a two-pronged nature of stereotypes about other groups of people. As Spencer-Rodgers (2001) noted:

> stereotypes have been conceptualized as culturally shared beliefs about the attributes that characterize a group of people (consensual, cultural, or social stereotypes) and in terms of unique, personal beliefs about the attributes of a group (individual, personal, or idiosyncratic stereotypes).
>
> (p. 642)

Studies of stereotypes as individually held beliefs usually focus on a person's ability "to perceive, remember, plan, and act" (Banaji, 2001, p. 15102). In other words, the researchers' main interests are the mental mechanics and cognitive processes that underlie stereotype formation, maintenance and change at the level of individual people. The research area that links mental mechanics involved in stereotyping to the way people act is known as the stereotype process (Banaji, 2001). Studies on the stereotype process do not overly concern themselves with whether there exists a prior social consensus regarding a set of stereotypes (Hamilton et al., 1994). However, in earlier stereotype research (e.g., Katz and Braly, 1933, 1935), the social processes take precedence over the workings of an individual person's mind (see Gardner, MacIntyre and Lalonde, 1995, p. 467). In this strand of psychological research, stereotypes are viewed as "culturally salient entities" (Blum, 2004, p. 252). To elucidate, Blum (2004) gives a somewhat tongue-in-cheek example of a Jim who, based on his personal experiences, forms an opinion that Finnish Americans are dishonest. This personal belief serves as a stereotype, a cognitive device, to Jim to the extent that he readily retrieves it whenever he meets a Finnish American. However, as Blum points out, "there is (as far as I am aware) no cultural stereotype of Finnish-Americans as dishonest" (p. 253). Thus, Jim's personal "picture in the head" of Finnish Americans is not culturally salient: it is not shared by other people.

The opinion that stereotypes that are commonly shared by larger groups of people have more legitimacy compared to idiosyncratic mental images held by individuals has been gaining some ground in psychology research (Schneider, 2005). As Bar-Tal (1997) observed, "Although stereotypes are formed, held and changed by individuals, their essential meaning and implication emerge only in the context of group membership because individuals' aggregation into groups serves as a basis for stereotyping" (p. 492). Stereotypes that are shared by a group of people – as opposed to mental images and beliefs held by an individual person – are referred to as "consensual, cultural or social stereotypes" (Spencer-Rodgers, 2001, p. 642). In this book, the term "consensual stereotype" is used. A stereotype is considered consensual if this particular image is shared by two or more learners of an Asian language. These consensual stereotypes are of particular interest to this study.

An overview of methodological approaches in research on stereotypes

Despite a lack of an overarching formal theory of stereotypes in psychology research, the methodological rigour of psychology studies on stereotypes is commendable. As Banaji (2001) noted, "When searching for large-scale theories of stereotypes or theories in which the role of stereotypes is central, one comes up relatively empty-handed"; however, she proceeds, the diversity in the research methods "in which stereotypes have been measured" compensates for the paucity of theoretical development (p. 15101).

In order to explore language learners' stereotypes of the six Asian target language countries, this book adopts several methodological techniques and approaches from psychology research. The following sections give an overview of the methodological problems faced by researchers and discusses some possible solutions to these problems. The discussion covers such areas as having to choose between structured and unstructured approaches to investigating stereotype content; the need for benchmarking or establishing a degree of consensus to distinguish when a stereotype becomes a stereotype; and assessing stereotype favourability or valence which helps to reveal attitudes embedded in the stereotypical images (Spencer-Rodgers, 2001, p. 641).

Exploring stereotype content: structured and unstructured approaches

Researchers recognize that "different measurement techniques may yield distinct stereotype profiles" (Spencer-Rodgers, 2001, p. 642). In psychology research, there exist structured and unstructured approaches to exploring stereotype content or what a stereotype consists of. The former includes the checklist technique, the percentage technique, respondents' answers to closed-ended items on the questionnaire forms, and so on, while the latter relies on data gathered as free-responses to open-ended questions in the research instruments. The following sections give more detailed explanations of these techniques.

Structured approaches: check-lists and percentage estimates

The check-list technique was introduced in research on stereotypes by Katz and Braly (1933). The researchers gave their respondents copies of a list that contained 84 adjectives describing individual people's personal traits and characteristics (e.g., "intelligent", "jovial", "scientifically-minded", "unreliable") and asked them to assign these traits to a number of selected ethnic and national groups. The percentage technique was developed by Brigham (1971) who asked respondents in his study to estimate the percentage of people within an ethnic or national group who possess a certain trait (e.g., "What percentage of Italian people are romantic?"). In other words, in the structured approaches, the researcher determines the lists of traits or qualities associated with the group of people, objects or phenomena under study.

There are advantages and disadvantages to employing structured methods. The advantages include a relative ease of analyzing the data, the presence of a clear structure in the findings and a high degree of consensus among the participants because they respond to the same set of questionnaire items. Another benefit is an enhanced possibility to make meaningful comparisons across the studies that employ the same research instrument. The main drawback of the structured approach is that the findings can be a function of the words or items that are included in the list. In other words, the findings may not reflect the respondents' own ideas and their mental representations of the object under study. Ehrlich and Rinehart's (1965) study may serve as a poignant example. The researchers demonstrated that people might assign qualities and characteristics to social or national groups even if they had never encountered them. In their study, Ehrlich and Rinehart distributed the Katz–Braly check-list to half of the respondents; the other half were asked to describe each of the target groups by writing as many words, adjectives or traits as they thought they needed. Besides the well-known

16 Stereotypes as a research focus

national groups, such as Americans, Russians and Japanese, the researchers included in their study the Alorese. As Ehrlich and Rinehart found out, none of the participants had reported a prior knowledge of the Alorese. However, those respondents who had received the closed-ended questionnaires proceeded to endorse 197 traits of the Alorese, while the participants who had been asked to provide their own descriptions of this group had generated 22 character traits to describe the Alorese.

Unstructured approaches: the free-response technique

An alternative way to collecting data on stereotypes is known as the free-response technique or free-listing. It is widely used in ethnographic and anthropological linguistic research. Free-response techniques are indispensable when there is little or no prior knowledge about stereotypes or cognitive representations of the study object. Even Katz and Braly's (1933) check-list of 84 adjectives used in their famous study was compiled from the free-response answers given by their participants in an earlier study. In the free-listing data collection approach, the respondents are typically asked either "to list all words, adjectives, or traits which they needed to adequately describe each target group" (Ehrlich and Rinehart, 1965, p. 566) or to list "all Xs that you know" about a topic (Sutrop, 2001; Weller and Romney, 1988).

The study of language learners' country stereotypes presented in this book adopted the free-response technique to collecting the students' mental images of six Asian target language countries. The main advantage of this approach is that the data yield the respondents' endogenous mental images or stereotypes that are most strongly associated with the research object in the minds of the respondents (see also Ehrlich and Rinehart, 1965; Niemann, Jennings, Rozelle, Baxter and Sullivan, 1994; Spencer-Rodgers, 2001). In addition, the free-response techniques are especially propitious for studies that aim to investigate consensual stereotypes rather than individually held mental images (Niemann et al., 1994), which is among the objectives of this book. Importantly, this is the best approach to adopt for research endeavours that aim to explore the contents of less-known stereotypes and the structure of these stereotypical images (Stangor and Lange, 1994). For example, some of the freely-recalled mental images would tend to readily appear in the respondents' minds and, as a result, they will be placed at the top of their lists of images, while other, less readily available images would be written at the bottom of the inventories. The sequence in which people recall and write down their mental images can be used for assessing salience or prominence of the stereotypical representations of the study object in the respondents' collective mind (Smith, Furbee, Maynard, Quick and Ross, 1995). The free-response technique is particularly suitable for the current

Stereotypes as a research focus 17

study because among its objectives is not only exploring the content and structure of the language learners' stereotypes but also assessing the salience of these images.

Among shortcomings associated with the free-response methods, Spencer-Rodgers (2001) mentions a possibility that respondents might omit some of the important traits associated with the research object if these traits do not immediately come to their minds. Also, the lists of traits produced as free-responses could be shorter compared to the trait inventories presented as check-lists, and there could be many idiosyncratic responses among the freely recalled items. All of this could make the process of coding, analyzing and interpreting the data more challenging and could yield findings that are less definitive and conclusive.

Measuring stereotypes: criteria for consensus

Measuring a degree of consensus concerning stereotype content not only yields valuable insights into the mental image's structure but also helps to establish whether the image is a consensual stereotype. However, there is no indisputably accepted benchmark for the consensus. In previous studies, researchers recognized a stereotype as consensual when "a substantial percentage" of the participants had mentioned this particular image (Spencer-Rodgers, 2001, p. 643). This "substantial percentage" ranged in various studies between 6% and 10%, and an even higher cut-off point could be adopted when the number of participants in a study was large. Applied linguistics research that focuses on language learners in a particular language classroom tends to have smaller numbers of participants; therefore, the researchers might want to adopt a lower benchmark for determining consensual stereotypes.

Assessing stereotype valence and salience

Researchers recognize that stereotypes are evaluative by nature, and attitudes embedded in stereotypical images can be positive, negative or neutral (Jones, 1997; Lippmann, 1922/1965; Spencer-Rodgers, 2001). Typically, the lists of adjectives that solicited data on national stereotypes in earlier studies contained both positive and negative personal traits and characteristics. For example, among the positive traits in the Katz–Braly list were "intelligent", "kind" and "courteous"; the negative traits included "lazy", "deceitful" and "unreliable" (Katz and Braly, 1933, p. 283). The problem with this approach is that while some traits would carry indisputably positive (or negative) connotations in various cultures, such as the words "kind" and "vicious" which, respectively, would be perceived as a positive and a negative personal quality, others characteristics can be more ambiguous (e.g., "conservative", "ambitious"). In some cultures, or even for some individual persons, the trait "ambitious" could denote a positive quality, while other people would consider this personal characteristic as negative. In addition, some personal traits can be viewed as neither positive nor negative. For example, while some people could consider the trait "sportsmanlike" as positive (or negative), other individuals may view this description as neutral. Clearly, all such evaluations are based on the respondents' subjective judgments and perceptions.

In studies that employ free-response techniques to collecting data on stereotypes, the participants are usually asked to, firstly, come up with their own sets of mental images about the study object and, secondly, to assign to each mental image a mark within a given range (e.g., from −3 to +3) (Madon et al., 2001; Nikitina and Furuoka, 2013a, 2013b, 2013c; Spencer-Rodgers, 2001). These marks are known as valence ratings or favourability ratings. This book will use the terms "favourability" interchangeably with the term "valence" in order to avoid an oxymoron "negative favourability". Valence is defined as the direction of a language learner's attitude and can be positive, negative or neutral.

As to stereotype salience, which refers to qualities of being important, noticeable, prominent and familiar, the more salient mental images would tend to promptly "pop up" in the minds of people. As a result, these images would be placed higher in the respondents' lists of images (Nikitina, 2017a; Weller and Romney, 1988). In contrast, the least salient images are those that come as an "afterthought", and for this reason they would tend to appear closer to the bottom or in the very end of the respondents' inventories. Several techniques have been developed to measure the salience of items in free lists (i.e., Smith, 1993; Smith et al., 1995; Sutrop, 2001). These approaches could be effectively applied in research on stereotypes and mental images held by people. However, a search of literature revealed that prior to my own explorations of language learners' mental images of target language countries (Nikitina and Furuoka, 2013a, 2013b) this approach was not adopted by researchers.

Thus far, this chapter has discussed issues in stereotype research predominantly from a social psychology perspective. This angle is appropriate since the main bulk of the research has been conducted by social psychologists. Albeit narrower in scope, some studies on the construct have been conducted by applied linguists and language educators who are interested in language learners' mental images of target language countries. The following sections give an overview of these studies and suggest how applied linguistics can contribute to the interdisciplinary scholarship on stereotypes.

Research on country stereotypes in applied linguistics

When people begin learning a foreign language, they usually would have a variety of "pictures in the head" of a target language country, its cultures and people. As Steele and Suozzo (1994) noted, "Unless students are encountering an absolutely exotic culture, they already reach the classroom with an array of stereotypes" (cited in Allen, 2004, p. 235). Researchers and language educators recognize that these stereotypes do not stem from language learners' thorough knowledge of a target language country. Rather, these mental images reflect perceptions, opinions, beliefs and attitudes prevalent in the language learners' social and cultural milieus. They are also aware that these stereotypes can influence people's choice of a foreign language to learn, and they could have an impact on the outcome of a language learning endeavour (Castellotti and Moore, 2002; Chaput, 1997; Gardner and Lambert, 1972; Heinzmann, 2013; Nikitina, 2019).

Research on stereotypes in the field of applied linguistics dates back to the 1970s (e.g., Taylor, 1977). Such studies have yielded some valuable insights and important implications for foreign language pedagogy. A review of scholarly literature has revealed that applied linguists and foreign language educators agree that the main problem with stereotypes that language learners bring into the classroom is not that these mental images are inherently negative or false. The main concern is that such stereotypes, being reductionist and inflexible by nature, restrict the students' views of the target culture to trivial and simplistic notions (Dlaska, 2000; Nikitina and Furuoka, 2013b; Schulz and Haerle, 1995; Webber, 1990). Language instructors recognize that their mission as educators is not limited to developing students' linguistic knowledge and communicative competencies; enhancing and deepening the language learners' understanding of the target culture is one of the main aims of foreign language teaching (Kelly, 1969/1976). Many studies have offered guidelines as to how language educators could effectively employ their students' country stereotypes to enhance the learners' cultural knowledge (Abrams, 2002; Allen, 2004; Byram and Kramsch, 2008; Houghton, 2010; Nikitina, 2017a; Nikitina and Furuoka, 2019). While making significant contributions to pedagogical repertoire, the geographical coverage of these studies is rather limited. The following section discusses this and other limitations of the available research on language learners' country stereotypes.

Research focus, aims, methodologies and gaps in studies on stereotypes held by language learners

Despite a considerable interest that applied linguists and language educators have accorded to stereotypes and mental images that language learners bring into the classroom, such explorations are still narrow in scope. In addition, insufficient attention has been given to methodological choices and theoretical perspectives from which a psychological construct of stereotypes could be explored. To be more specific, the overwhelming number of these studies has been done in Western educational contexts and predominantly among learners of European languages (Abrams, 2002; Allen, 2004; Drewelow, 2013; Heinzmann, 2013; Schulz and Haerle, 1995; Salak and Durdević, 2017; Storme and Derakhshani, 2002; Taylor, 1977; Webber, 1990). Only recently, research on country stereotypes has been initiated among language learners in Asian countries. Nonetheless, with the exception of very few studies (Nikitina, 2019; Nikitina and Furuoka, 2013b, 2019), the focus of these scholarly investigations has remained on the learners of European languages.

As to the research aims, for the most part, studies on language learners' country and national stereotypes have been pedagogically motivated. In other words, they were done in order to, firstly, raise the language educators' awareness of the presence of implicit stereotypical notions in the students' perceptions and, secondly, to introduce effective pedagogical approaches to the teaching of the target culture and expanding the learners' cultural knowledge (Abrams, 2002; Drewelow, 2013; Houghton, 2010; Nikitina, 2017a; Webber, 1990). The importance of this research vector cannot be overestimated. However, the strong pedagogical motivation of these studies might have undermined their methodological rigour: because the researchers were mostly interested in the stereotype content, they had collected exclusively qualitative data. Among the earliest studies, Taylor (1977) collected qualitative data on the respondents' knowledge of German-speaking countries, geographical areas in Germany and their perceptions of Germany's past and present. In Schulz and Haerle's (1995) study, the students were asked to complete the phrase *"Die Deutschen . . ."* ("The Germans . . ."), which yielded a wealth of information in the form of qualitative data. While employing qualitative approaches to collecting and analyzing the data was entirely appropriate to meet the studies' research objectives, such analyses did not fully utilize rich affordances of the qualitative methodology. For example, they made no attempts to assess the salience of the language learners' stereotypical images.

Also lacking were systematic assessments of a degree of consensus in language learners' stereotypical representations of target language countries. Furthermore, notwithstanding the fact that assessments of stereotype valence would provide critical information for language educators, the assessments of attitudes embedded in students' country images and stereotypes were done in a heuristic manner. For example, Schulz and Haerle (1995) concluded that their respondents' images of Germany and German people were mostly positive. However, some of the mental images that the authors identified as positive might be evaluated as neutral or even negative by other people. Such images included character traits "*stolz*" (meaning "proud") and "*mit viel Gefühl*" ("with much feeling", "emotional", "expressive").

Another gap in applied linguistics research on country and national stereotypes in the context of language teaching and learning is that, until recently, no attempts have been made to examine links between these mental images and language learners' L2 motivation. It should be noted that the capacity of stereotypes, and attitudes embedded in them, to influence L2 motivation was acknowledged by Gardner and Lambert (1972) in their influential book *Attitudes and Motivation in Second Language Learning*. However, the researchers did not proceed to explore the endogenous country stereotypes held by language learners. More recently, Heinzmann (2013) assessed associations between country stereotypes and L2 motivation in her study among young German-speaking Swiss learners of English and French. However, the data on stereotypes were obtained through the closed-ended questionnaire items and, therefore, might not reflect the respondents' endogenous perceptions. Furthermore, the data on stereotypes were collected from only a fraction of the respondents and not from the entire group of the language learners involved in the study.

In conclusion, the ubiquity of stereotypes in our daily lives, including in the foreign language classroom, the function of stereotypes as an indispensable cognitive tool and their ability to influence our actions have resulted in researchers' lasting interest in this psychological construct. The scholarship on stereotypes has been interdisciplinary in nature, with many academic fields contributing to our better understanding of this phenomenon. Applied linguistics research on country and national stereotypes has yielded some useful insights. Notwithstanding, the contribution of the discipline remains minimal. Applied linguistics stands at the conflux of several academic fields and is well positioned to expand the existing knowledge on stereotypes. Especially in view that though stereotype formation and maintenance involve social processes and engage cognitive mechanisms, which has been extensively researched in psychology, such mental images would need to be firstly *verbalized* in order to become generalized and shared by a group of people. This book proposes that adopting Vygotskian linguistically saturated concepts of word meaning (*znachenie slova*) and word sense (*smysl*) could be a promising direction for applied linguistics research on stereotypes. Chapter 2 offers a more detailed discussion of these and other main constructs in this study. It also proposes how empirical linkages can be established between language learners' country stereotypes and their L2 motivation.

References

Abrams, Z. I. (2002). Surfing to cross-cultural awareness: Using Internet-mediated projects to explore cultural stereotypes. *Foreign Language Annals, 35*(2), 141–160. doi: 10.1111/j.1944-9720.2002.tb03151.x

Allen, L. Q. (2004). Implementing a culture portfolio project within a constructivist paradigm. *Foreign Language Annals, 37*(2), 232–239. doi: 10.1111/j.1944-9720.2004.tb02196.x

Allport, G. W. (1954). *The nature of prejudice*. Cambridge, MA: Addison–Wesley Publishing Company.

Ashmore, R. D., & Del Boca, F. K. (1979). Sex stereotypes and implicit personality theory: Toward a cognitive-social psychological conceptualization. *Sex Roles, 5*(2), 219–248.

Banaji, M. R. (2001). Stereotypes, social psychology of. In N. J. Smelser & P. B. Baltes (Eds.), *International encyclopedia of the social and behavioral sciences* (pp. 15100–15104). Oxford: Pergamon.

Bar-Tal, D. (1997). Formation and change of ethnic and national stereotypes: An integrative model. *International Journal of Intercultural Relations, 21*(4), 491–523. http://dx.doi.org/10.1016/S0147-1767(97)00022-9

Blum, L. (2004). Stereotypes and stereotyping: A moral analysis. *Philosophical Papers, 33*(3), 251–289.

Boulding, K. E. (1959). National images and international systems. *The Journal of Conflict Resolution, 3*(2), 120–131.

Brigham, J. C. (1971). Racial stereotypes, attitudes, and evaluations of and behavioral intentions toward Negroes and whites. *Sociometry, 34*(3), 360–380.

Brijs, K., Bloemer, J., & Kasper, H. (2011). Country-image discourse model: Unraveling meaning, structure, and function of country images. *Journal of Business Research, 64*(12), 1259–1269. doi: 10.1016/j.jbusres.2011.01.017

Byram, K., & Kramsch, C. (2008). Why is it so difficult to teach language as culture? *The German Quarterly, 81*(1), 20–34. doi: 10.2307/27676139

Castellotti, V., & Moore, D. (2002). *Social representations of languages and teaching: Guide for the development of language education policies in Europe from linguistic diversity to plurilingual education*. Strasbourg: Council of Europe.

Chaput, P. R. (1997). Culture in grammar. *The Slavic and East European Journal, 41*, 403–414. doi: 10.2307/310183

Clark, T. (1990). International marketing and national character: A review and proposal for an integrative theory. *Journal of Marketing, 54*(4), 66–79. doi: 10.2307/1251760

De Luca Braun, R. (2003). *Made in Hollywood: Italian stereotypes in the movies*. Retrieved September 12, 2013, from www.osia.org/documents/Made-in-Hollywood.pdf

Dlaska, A. (2000). Integrating culture and language learning in institution-wide language programmes. *Language, Culture and Curriculum, 13*(3), 247–263. doi: 10.1080/07908310008666602

Drewelow, I. (2013). Impact of instruction on shaping or reshaping stereotypical cultural representations in an introductory French course. *Foreign Language Annals, 46*(2), 157–174. doi: 10.1111/flan.12029

Echtner, C. M., & Ritchie, J. R. B. (1993). The measurement of destination image: An empirical assessment. *Journal of Travel Research, 31*(4), 3–13.

Ehrlich, H. J., & Rinehart, J. W. (1965). A brief report on the methodology of stereotype research. *Social Forces, 43*(4), 564–575.

Enesco, I., Navarro, A., Paradela, I., & Guerrero, S. (2005). Stereotypes and beliefs about different ethnic groups in Spain: A study with Spanish and Latin American children living in Madrid. *Journal of Applied Developmental Psychology, 26*(6), 638–659. doi: 10.1016/j.appdev.2005.08.009

Gardner, R. C., & Lambert, W. E. (1972). *Attitudes and motivation in second-language learning.* Rowley, MA: Newbury House Publishers.

Gardner, R. C., MacIntyre, P. D., & Lalonde, R. N. (1995). The effects of multiple social categories on stereotyping. *Canadian Journal of Behavioural Science, 27*(4), 466–483.

Hamilton, D. L., Stroessner, S. J., & Driscoll, D. M. (1994). Social cognition and the study of stereotyping. In P. G. Devine, D. L. Hamilton, & T. M. Ostrom (Eds.), *Social cognition: Impact on social psychology* (pp. 291–321). San Diego, CA: Academic Press.

Harding, J., Proshansky, H., Kutner, B., & Chein, I. (1969). Prejudice and ethnic relations. In G. Lindzey & E. Aronson (Eds.), *Handbook of social psychology* (2nd ed., Vol. 5, pp. 1–76). Reading, MA: Addison-Wesley.

Heinzmann, S. (2013). *Young language learners' motivation and attitudes: Longitudinal, comparative and explanatory perspectives.* New York, NY: Bloomsbury.

Herz, M., & Diamantopoulos, A. (2013). Activation of country stereotypes: automaticity, consonance, and impact. *Journal of the Academy of Marketing Science, 41*(4), 400–417. doi: 10.1007/s11747-012-0318-1

Houghton, S. (2010). Managing stereotypes through experiential learning. *Intercultural Communication Studies, 19*(1), 182–198.

Jones, J. M. (1997). *Prejudice and racism* (2nd ed.). New York, NY: McGraw-Hill.

Katz, D., & Braly, K. W. (1933). Racial stereotypes of one hundred college students. *Journal of Abnormal Psychology, 28*(3), 280–290.

Katz, D., & Braly, K. W. (1935). Racial prejudice and racial stereotypes. *The Journal of Abnormal and Social Psychology, 30*(2), 175–193.

Kelly, L. G. (1969/1976). *25 centuries of language teaching.* Rowley, MA: Newbury House Publishers.

Lambert, W. E., & Klineberg, O. (1967). *Children's views of foreign people.* New York, NY: Appleton-Century-Crofts.

Leerssen, J. (2003). *Images-information-national identity and national stereotype.* Retrieved August 12, 2013, from http://cf.hum.uva.nl/images/info/leers.html

Lindsay, I. (1997). *The uses and abuses of national stereotypes.* Unit for the Study of Government, Department of Politics, University of Edinburgh. Retrieved July 12, 2013, from www.scottishaffairs.org/backiss/pdfs/sa20/SA20_Lindsay.pdf

Lippmann, W. (1922/1965). *Public opinion.* New York, NY: The Free Press.

Mackie, M. M. (1973). Arriving at "truth" by definition: The case of stereotype inaccuracy. *Social Problems, 20*, 431–447.

Madon, S., Guyll, M., Aboufadel, K., Montiel, E., Smith, A., Palumbo, P., & Jussim, L. (2001). Ethnic and national stereotypes: The Princeton Trilogy revisited and revised. *Personality and Social Psychology Bulletin, 27*(8), 996–1010. doi: 10.1177/0146167201278007

McCrae, R. R., & Terracciano, A. (2006). National character and personality. *Current Directions in Psychological Science, 15*(4), 156–161. doi: 10.1111/j.1467-8721.2006.00427.x

Messick, D. M., & Mackie, D. M. (1989). Intergroup relations. *Annual Review of Psychology, 40*, 45–81.

Niemann, Y. F., Jennings, L., Rozelle, R. M., Baxter, J. C., & Sullivan, E. (1994). Use of free responses and cluster analysis to determine stereotypes of eight groups. *Personality and Social Psychology Bulletin, 20*(4), 379–390. doi: 10.1177/0146167294204005

Nikitina, L. (2017a). Language learners' representations of Spanish-speaking countries: How can they inform language pedagogy? Las representaciones de los aprendices de una lengua sobre los países hablantes de español:¿ Cómo pueden ellos informar sobre la pedagogía de la lengua? *Revista Signos, 50*(93), 50–70. doi: 10.4067/S0718-09342017000100003

Nikitina, L. (2017b). Stereotypes as an interdisciplinary construct: Implications for applied linguistics research. *Suvremena lingvistika, 43*(83), 1–19. doi: 10.22210/suvlin.2017.083.01

Nikitina, L. (2019). Do country stereotypes influence language learning motivation? A study among foreign language learners in Malaysia. *Moderna Språk, 113*(1), 58–79.

Nikitina, L., & Furuoka, F. (2013a). "A distant land of snow . . .": Russian language learners' representations of Russia. *Zeitschrift für Slawistik, 58*(2), 193–204.

Nikitina, L., & Furuoka, F. (2013b). "Dragon, kung fu and Jackie Chan . . .": Stereotypes about China held by Malaysian students. *Trames-Journal of the Humanities and Social Sciences, 17*(2), 175–195. doi: 10.3176/tr.2013.2.05

Nikitina, L., & Furuoka, F. (2013c). Podobe države in stereotipi, kijih o Rusih gojijo učenci ruskega jezika [Country images and stereotypes about Russia held by learners of Russian]. *Slavistična Revija, 61*(2), 432–438.

Nikitina, L., & Furuoka, F. (2019). Language learners' mental images of Korea: Insights for the teaching of culture in the language classroom. *Journal of Multilingual and Multicultural Development, 40*(9), 774–786. doi: 10.1080/01434632.2018.1561704

Oskamp, S., & Schultz, P. W. (2005). *Attitudes and opinions* (3rd ed.). Mahwah, NJ: Lawrence Erlbaum Associates.

Oxford English Dictionary (1991). Oxford: Oxford University Press.

Piaget, J., & Weil, A. M. (1951). The development in children of the idea of the homeland and of relations with other countries. *International Social Sciences Bulletin: National Stereotypes and International Understanding, 3*(3), 561–578.

Realo, A., Allik, J., Lönnqvist, J.-E., Verkasalo, M., Kwiatkowska, A., Kööts, L., & Renge, V. (2009). Mechanisms of the national character stereotype: How people in six neighbouring countries of Russia describe themselves and the typical Russian. *European Journal of Personality, 23*(3), 229–249. doi: 10.1002/per.719

Robins, R. W. (2005). The nature of personality: Genes, culture, and national character. *Science, 310*(5745), 62–63. doi: 10.2307/3842856

Rudmin, F. W. (1989). The pleasure of serendipity in historical research: On finding "stereotype" in Morier's (1924) Hajji Baba. *Cross Cultural Psychology Bulletin, 23*(2), 8–11.

Salak, T., & Durdević, R. (2017). Kako me vidiš? Predodžbe neizvornih govornika hrvatskoga o Hrvatskoj i Hrvatima. (How do you see me? Ideas of non-native Croatian speakers about Croatia and Croats) (in Croatian). *Filološke Studije*, *15*(1), 243–259.

Schneider, D. J. (2005). *The psychology of stereotyping*. New York: The Guilford Press.

Schulz, R. A., & Haerle, B. M. (1995). "Beer, fast cars, and...": Stereotypes held by U.S. college-level students of German. *Die Unterrichtspraxis/Teaching German*, *28*(1), 29–39.

Shaheen, J. G. (2003). Reel bad Arabs: How Hollywood vilifies a people. *Annals of the American Academy of Political and Social Science*, *588*, 171–193. doi: 10.2307/1049860

Skubikowski, U. (1985). Understanding contemporary Italy: Supplementing texts in beginning Italian. *The Modern Language Journal*, *69*(1), 35–40. doi: 10.2307/327877

Smith, D. S. (1973). Mass communications and international image change. *The Journal of Conflict Resolution*, *17*(1), 115–129.

Smith, J. J. (1993). Using ANTHROPAC 3.5 and a spreadsheet to compute a free-list salience index. *Cultural Anthropology Methods*, *5*(3), 1–3.

Smith, J. J., Furbee, L., Maynard, K., Quick, S., & Ross, L. (1995). Salience counts: A domain analysis of English color terms. *Journal of Linguistic Anthropology*, *5*(2), 203–216.

Spencer-Rodgers, J. (2001). Consensual and individual stereotypic beliefs about international students among American host nationals. *International Journal of Intercultural Relations*, *25*(6), 639–657. doi: 10.1016/S0147-1767(01)00029-3

Stangor, C., & Lange, J. E. (1994). Mental representations of social groups: Advances in understanding stereotypes and stereotyping. In M. P. Zanna (Ed.), *Advances in experimental social psychology* (pp. 357–416). London: Academic Press.

Steele, R., and Suozzo, A. (1994). *Teaching French culture: Theory and practice*. Lincolnwood, IL: National Textbook Co.

Stephan, W. G. (1985). Intergroup relations. In G. Lindzey & E. Aronson (Eds.), *Handbook of social psychology* (3rd ed., Vol. 2, pp. 599–658). New York: Random House.

Storme, J. A., & Derakhshani, M. (2002). Defining, teaching, evaluating cultural and proficiency in the foreign language classroom. *Foreign Language Annals*, *35*(6), 657–668.

Sutrop, U. (2001). List task and a cognitive salience index. *Field Methods*, *13*(3), 263–276. doi: 10.1177/1525822x0101300303

Taylor, I. C. (1977). Beware of cultural clichés. *Die Unterrichtspraxis/Teaching German*, *10*(2), 108–114. doi: 10.2307/3529799

Terracciano, A., Abdel-Khalek, A. M., Ádám, N., Adamovová, L., Ahn, C.-K., Ahn, H.-N., & McCrae, R. R. (2005). National character does not reflect mean personality trait levels in 49 cultures. *Science*, *310*(5745), 96–100. doi: 10.1126/science.1117199

Webber, M. J. (1990). Intercultural stereotypes and the teaching of German. *Die Unterrichtspraxis/Teaching German*, *23*(2), 132–141.

Weller, S. C., & Romney, A. K. (1988). *Systematic data collection*. Beverly Hills, CA: Sage Publications.

2 Motivation, attitudes and stereotypes in L2 research
Connecting the dots

Motivation in applied linguistics research: an overview of literature

The term "motivation" originates from the Latin word *motus*, which had an original meaning of "a moving, motion". Early in the 20th century, the term acquired the meaning "inner or social stimulus for an action" ("Motivation", 2013), which has become recognized as a key feature of the construct of motivation. As Ryan and Deci (2000) noted, "to be motivated means *to be moved* to do something" (p. 54, italics in the original). Motivation is a complex psychological construct. It has been theorized from various perspectives and operationalized in various ways. Notwithstanding the multitude of the definitions, three main attributes of motivation are "the direction and magnitude of human behaviour", "the persistence with it" and "the effort expanded on it" (Dörnyei, 2001, p. 8).

In the context of second language education, the first systematic theory of L2 motivation was developed by Canadian social psychologists Robert C. Gardner and Wallace E. Lambert (1959). The theory incorporated two influential concepts – "integrative orientation" and "instrumental orientation" – which concerned the main goals that "move" or propel language learners into action. The instrumental orientation was defined as "a desire to gain social recognition or economic advantage through knowledge of a foreign language", while the integrative orientation was conceived as a language learner's desire to emulate or "become associated" with the speakers of the target language (Gardner and Lambert, 1972, p. 14). A few decades later Gardner (1985) formalized his socio-educational model of L2 motivation which provided a solid theoretical framework and afforded methodological rigor to numerous consequent studies on language learning motivation. However, it should be noted that since the 1970s, the notion of "integrativeness" embedded in the integrative orientation has received much criticism from researchers and language educators who argued that the intention of being "associated" with the target language-speaking community may not be applicable to each and every learning context. For example, as some researchers maintained, the "integrative orientation" might be lacking in the context of learning a *foreign* language, especially when there are considerable geographical, cultural or ideological distances and differences between the language learners' own country and the target language country. This debate underscored the need for a more encompassing definition of the integrative orientation. In his more recent writings, Gardner (2010) suggested – and the current book shares this viewpoint – that definitions of the integrative orientation should incorporate language learners' favourable interest toward the target language country, its language, cultures and people.

The criticisms of the Gardnerian model of L2 motivation have led to shifts in the theoretical underpinnings of research on L2 motivation. One of the most notable theoretical developments occurred in the 2000s when Zoltán Dörnyei (2005) introduced the L2 Motivational Self System framework (L2MSS). His model was rooted in the theory of possible selves (Markus and Nurius, 1986) and self-discrepancy theory (Higgins, 1987) developed in the field of psychology. The available quantitative L2 research within the L2MSS framework has mostly focused on two dimensions of L2 self – the ideal L2 Self (i.e., a desirable future self-image) and ought-to L2 Self (i.e., the range of attributes the language learner believes he or she must possess). At the same time, the feared self – a key concept in the original self-discrepancy theory (Higgins, 1987) – remains underexplored and less clearly defined in L2 research (Yu, Brown and Stephens, 2018).

Despite a growing prominence of the L2MSS model in research literature, it appears that while the model realigns the focus of research on L2 motivation toward language learners' imagery and perceptions of their L2 self, including the "interpersonal" L2 self that needs to live up to the expectations from one's social milieu (e.g., family and friends), the model does not explicitly consider language learners' "intercultural L2 self". This could undermine the applicability of the L2MSS in the contexts of foreign language learning because language learners' intercultural stance, the beliefs about and attitudes toward a target language country, its cultures and people are important aspects of motivation to learn a foreign language. For example, people often choose a particular foreign language to learn and keep persevering in their language learning endeavours due to their personal fascination with a target language country and its cultures (Chaput, 1997; Dlaska, 2000). To deal with this gap in the L2MSS framework, researchers adapt and include in their studies the questionnaire scales that assess the integrative orientation and their respondents' attitudes toward the target language community (Busse, 2013; Gearing and Roger, 2019; Islam, Lamb and Chambers, 2013). This fact attests that despite all the criticisms, the construct of integrative orientation has retained a strong intellectual appeal and has a considerable empirical usefulness for studies on L2 motivation. Recognizing its theoretical and empirical value, the current study adopts the Gardnerian socio-educational model of L2 motivation. It defines L2 motivation as the effort and perseverance that students are willing to expend to learn a target language to achieve their goals, plus a favourable interest in and positive attitudes toward a target language country, its cultures, people and the language itself. The current study proposes that stereotypes that learners of the six Asian languages have of the target language countries would have relationships with their L2 motivation. The link could be especially prominent in the case of the integrative orientation. This assumption was made based on the theoretical underpinnings (Gardner and Lambert, 1959, 1972) and findings from earlier empirical studies among learners of European languages that had detected statistically significant and strong associations between the two constructs (Nikitina, 2015, 2019).

Goal setting in language learning: instrumental and integrative orientations

A hallmark of a motivated behaviour is the pursuit of a goal. Goals are often referred to as "orientations" in psychology research. As Ryan and Deci (2000) explained, "Orientation of motivation concerns the underlying attitudes and goals that give rise to action – that is, it concerns the why of actions" (p. 54). Psychologists distinguish between two main motivational orientations – intrinsic and extrinsic. The former refers to "doing something because it is inherently interesting or enjoyable", while the latter comes into existence when people are "doing something because it leads to a separable outcome" (Ryan and Deci, 2000, p. 55). In other words, intrinsically motivated individuals engage in an activity for fun, pleasure, intellectual stimulation or challenge. When people are extrinsically motivated, they are moved to action because of external factors, such as, for example, being given financial rewards or receiving social recognition. The two orientations in the Gardnerian model of L2 motivation closely align with these conceptualizations.

To be more specific, in their pioneering study among learners of French in a Canadian high school, Gardner and Lambert (1959) described the learners as "integratively oriented" if the students agreed that good knowledge of French "would be helpful in understanding the French–Canadian people and their way of life", and that good language proficiency would "permit meeting and conversing with more and varied people" (p. 268). As Gardner (1985) explained later, "These two reasons for learning French were classified as integrative because they appeared to stress interaction with members of the French speaking community for social-emotional purposes" (p. 11). While the earliest conceptualization of the integrative orientation pertained to the language learners' desire "to be like valued members of the language community" (p. 271), a wider definition given in Gardner's (1985) later work described the integrative orientation as a "class of reasons that suggest that the individual is learning a second language in order to learn about, interact with, or become closer to, the second language community". He also acknowledged that "integrative orientation reflects a goal to learn a second language because of a favourable interest in the other language community" (p. 54). Clearly, since its inception, the construct of integrative orientation incorporated a prominent attitudinal aspect. Current definitions of the integrative orientation include various attitudinal dispositions on the part of language learners toward the target language country, its cultures and native speakers.

As Gardner (2010) noted, integrative orientation has come to be recognized as a complex and multilevel concept. On the extreme end of the spectrum, the integrative orientation, or integrativeness, can entail a complete self-identification with target language speakers. In a wider sense, integrative orientation involves a positive disposition toward and favourable interest in a target language country, its cultures and speaking community (Gardner, 2010). This shift in the theoretical perspective is reflected in more recent empirical investigations of L2 motivation that include not only language learners' attitudes toward a target language country, its cultures and people but also their desire to develop a deeper appreciation and better understanding of the target culture, arts and literature (Nikitina, 2015; Yang, 2003). In this book, the integrative orientation is viewed as a student's intention to learn a target language for the purposes of communicating with the speakers of this language and gaining a better understanding of the target language country, its cultures, people and their ways of life. The instrumental orientation in the current study is viewed as a language learner's intention to learn a target language for practical purposes, such as getting financial benefits and employment or study opportunities.

Due to a multitude of factors that influence the ebbs and flows of language learners' L2 motivation, statistical analyses in earlier studies of motivated language learning behaviour incorporated a miscellany of variables. This precludes a possibility of making a neat comparison across the findings of a voluminous body of literature. A brief overview of empirical findings in this section includes only studies that adopted the Gardnerian (1985) model of L2 motivation and that incorporated in their models measures of language learners' attitudes toward the target language countries and speaking communities. As one example, Csizér and Dörnyei (2005) investigated the internal structure of L2 motivation of Hungarian schoolchildren who learnt German, English, Italian, French and Russian. The researchers were particularly interested in the relationship between the language learners' L2 motivation, their choice of a foreign language and the efforts they were willing to expend to learn this language. To achieve their research aim, Csizér and Dörnyei included in their model the variables "vitality of the L2 community", "attitudes toward L2 speakers/community" and "cultural interest". Essentially, each of these variables measured the students' perceptions of the target language country, its culture and people. As the researchers explained, the variable "vitality of the L2 community" assessed "the perceived importance and wealth of the L2 communities in question", the variable "attitudes toward the L2 speakers/community" is self-explanatory, and the variable "cultural interest" assessed "the appreciation of cultural products associated with the particular L2" (pp. 21–22). A notable finding reported by Csizér and Dörnyei was that the language learners' attitudes toward L2 speakers acted as a direct antecedent of the integrative orientation. Furthermore, this variable was directly influenced by the variables "cultural interest" and "vitality of the L2 community". In another study, Csizér and Kormos (2009) employed the structural equation modelling technique to examine the effect of cross-cultural contacts on Hungarian schoolchildren's language attitudes and L2 motivation. The findings indicated that "language-related attitudes" was one of the two variables that directly affected the students' L2 motivation (Csizér and Kormos, 2009).

Despite abundant research on L2 motivation in various cultural and geographical contexts, including Malaysia (Ainol and Isarji, 2009; Aladdin, 2010; Tan, Ooi and Hairul, 2012), there is a lack of studies that examined the relationship between stereotypes or mental images that language learners have of the target language country and L2 motivation. Though the links between the constructs of stereotypes, language attitudes and L2 motivation were noted several decades ago (Gardner and Lambert, 1972) and, more recently, calls were made to empirically examine these links (Byon, 2007), there is a scarcity of studies that explore the endogenous stereotypes held by language learners and then proceed to examine the relationships between these mental images, the students' language attitudes and their L2 motivation in one research project. Some steps in this direction have been initiated, and empirical studies were conducted among learners of European languages (Heinzmann, 2013; Nikitina, 2015, 2019). However, up to date, no scholarly investigations on language learners' country images and L2 motivation have been done among learners of Asian languages. Before explaining how the links can be established between the language learners' endogenous country images, their language attitudes and L2 motivation, this chapter offers a brief overview of another key construct in this study – attitude.

The construct of attitude in psychology and applied linguistics

Attitude: etymology and definitions

Attitude is an inseparable part of a stereotype. Lippmann (1922/1965) has highlighted a close link between the two constructs in his observation that stereotypes are "highly charged with the feelings that are attached to them" (p. 64). Feelings are recognized by psychologists as "the most essential part of attitude" (Fishbein and Ajzen, 1975, p. 216). Though stereotypes have often been associated with prejudice, which is an unjustified and negative attitude, in fact stereotypes can have positive, negative or even neutral attitudes attached to them.

The term "attitude" originates from the Late Latin word *aptus* which means "joined, fitted" ("Attitude", 2013). The word "attitude" came to the English language in the 17th century via a French borrowing of the then contemporary Italian word, *attitudine*, which meant "disposition, posture" and "aptness". For a considerable period of time the word "attitude" remained a technical term to describe the posture of a figure or body in a work of art. Only in the 19th century did it acquire the meaning of a "settled behaviour reflecting feeling or opinion". Since then, the meaning of the word "attitude" has come to incorporate the notion of the "disposition" of a person's mind.

Attitude is one of the central and most researched constructs in psychology. In contrast to research on stereotypes, which is not guided by an overarching theory, studies on attitude are supported by a solid theoretical foundation. Similar to other major psychological constructs, attitude has been defined in a multitude of ways. The briefest definition was offered by Bem (1970) who described attitudes as "likes and dislikes" (cited in Oskamp and Schultz, 2005, p. 8). A broader definition was hammered out by Eagly and Chaiken (1993), who considered attitudes as "tendencies to evaluate an entity with some degree of favor or disfavor, ordinarily expressed in cognitive, affective, and behavioral responses" (p. 155). Commenting on a multitude of perspectives and angles from which researchers have approached the construct of attitude, Scott (1954/1968) pointed out that a definition of the construct would depend on a researcher's "own theoretical purposes – which may vary from one investigator to another" (p. 205). It should be noted, however, that definitions of an attitude in psychology studies would include and give prominence to its evaluative nature. In the current study, attitude is defined as a language learner's favourable or unfavourable disposition toward a target language country, its cultures and people. These attitudes are quantitatively measured by the valence ratings assigned by each student to his or her list of images of a target language country (see Chapter 3, which explains the instrumentation and methodology).

32   Motivation, attitudes and stereotypes

There is also a long-standing scholarly tradition to link the construct of attitude to cognition and behaviour. As Oskamp and Schultz (2005) noted, "This conceptual distinction among thoughts, feelings, and actions as separate but interrelated parts of an attitude has a long history in philosophy" (p. 10). The tripartite model of an attitude proposes that this construct subsumes three components, namely, affective, cognitive and conative. Oppenheim (1966/2004) provided the following explanation for this theoretical approach: "Attitudes are reinforced by beliefs (the cognitive component) and often attract strong feelings (the emotional component) which may lead to particular behavioural intents (the action tendency component" (p. 175). The tripartite structure of an attitude allows establishing theoretical links between the main three constructs of interest in the current study – stereotypes or mental images of the target language country (the cognitive component), feelings embedded in these images (the emotional component) and L2 motivation (the action tendency). Recognizing that the three components are enmeshed and intertwined, in this book attitudes are measured as language learners' feelings (the emotional aspect) embedded in their stereotypes (the cognitive aspect) of the target language country.

Research on attitudes in the field of applied linguistics

This study aims to introduce a rigorous approach to analyzing language learners' stereotypes of target language countries and attitudes embedded in these mental images. First of all, it is important to establish that in applied linguistics research, the term "attitudes" or "language attitudes" is not limited to the feelings and dispositions that language learners have toward the target language per se. In addition to these feelings, it encompasses the learners' attitudes toward, and beliefs about, the speakers of the target language (Kormos, Kiddle and Csizér, 2011; McKenzie, 2010) and to the country or countries where this language is spoken (Nikitina, 2015, 2019; Schulz and Haerle, 1995). Importantly, researchers recognize that language attitudes are influential "emotional precursors" of a language learning behaviour (Kormos et al., 2011, p. 497). Therefore, it would be logical to propose that attitudes embedded in language learners' mental images or stereotypes of a target language country would be an influential motivating factor in the process of learning an additional language.

As earlier studies have demonstrated (Chaput, 1997; Dlaska, 2000; Gardner and Lambert, 1959, 1972), language attitudes do play a prominent role in determining the choice of a foreign language to learn and in maintaining the learners' L2 motivation. Regarding the tripartite structure of an attitude, in the context of learning a foreign language, the affective component could transpire as language learners' feelings about a target language country, its cultures and people (e.g., "China is fantastic!"; "Japanese culture is awesome!"). The cognitive component would be reflected in the learners' beliefs about the target language country and people (e.g., "Japan is the cleanest country in the world"; "the Thais are beautiful people"). The conative aspect would shape the language learners' behaviour or their intentions to learn a particular language (e.g., "I love Chinese culture and want to learn Mandarin") or serve as a motivational orientation (e.g., "I like the Japanese and I want to work in Japan"; "I am learning Korean because I come to like the language through watching Korean dramas on the TV, and I want to understand what they say"). However, it appears that explorations of attitudes that explicitly focus on target language countries are scarce.

Stereotypes, attitudes and L2 motivation: connecting the dots

Russian psychologist Lev Vygotsky (1896–1934) proposed that psychological functions are not independent entities that exist in isolation: these functions and processes are involved in a net of complex systemic relationships with each other (see Kozulin, 1990). In a similar way, Buck (2005) maintained that "in their fully articulated forms, emotions imply cognitions imply motives imply emotions, and so on" (cited in Dörnyei and Ryan, 2015, p. 11). This book fully acknowledges and agrees with these postulates. As discussed earlier, stereotypes function as an important cognitive tool that enables individual people to process new information in a more effective way (Lippmann, 1922/1965; McGarty, Yzerbyt and Spears, 2002). In addition to being an indispensable cognitive device, stereotypes incorporate people's attitudes toward the stereotyped objects, social groups or phenomena (Greenwald and Banaji, 1995; Lippmann, 1922/1965; Spencer-Rodgers, 2001). Importantly, these attitudes can influence or shape people's behavioural intentions and guide their actions (Forbes and Schmader, 2010; Greenwald and Banaji, 1995).

This book considers an attitude as a property of a stereotype or as the language learners' "likes and dislikes" embedded in their mental images of the target language countries. These attitudes, as Chapter 3 will explain in more detail, are measured in this study by favourability ratings that the respondents attached to each stereotypical image they had provided in their lists of images. To connect the dots between the three constructs in this study – stereotypes, attitudes and L2 motivation – the recognition that stereotypes incorporate individual people's attitudes and have an ability to initiate a particular behaviour logically leads to a proposition that country stereotypes or mental images that language learners have about target language countries – and the learners' attitudes embedded in these images – would play a role in shaping the students' L2 motivation.

Numerous studies in the field of applied linguistics have explored mental images of target language countries and cultures held by language learners. The researchers acknowledged that these 'pictures in the head' would "undoubtedly elicit stereotypes"; these stereotypes, in their turn, would allow having some valuable insights into the language learners' attitudes toward the target language country, cultures and people (Storme and Derakhshani, 2002, p. 659). Methodologically, country stereotypes held by language learners have been explored through posing open-ended questions and gathering qualitative data. This approach was appropriate for the aims of the earlier studies, and it was employed by many researchers beginning from the earliest available inquiry by Taylor (1977) until more recent scholarly investigations by Byon (2007) and Drewelow (2013). However, the previous studies did not proceed to linking the explorations of the language learners' mental imagery of the target language country to the learners' language attitudes and L2 motivation. Only recently was such research initiated (Heinzmann, 2013; Nikitina, 2015). My own research conducted among learners of Brazilian Portuguese, Italian, French, German, European Portuguese, Russian and Spanish languages provided empirical evidence for the existence of positive and statistically significant associations between country stereotypes, language attitudes and L2 motivation (Nikitina, 2015). A study presented in the current book extends the explorations of the links between the three constructs to the learners of Asian languages. Besides extending the scope of the research, this book also recognizes that in order to enable methodological advancements in research on country stereotypes, a solid theoretical foundation would be required. The following section discusses some possible theoretical underpinnings.

How applied linguistics research can contribute to the scholarship on stereotypes

Applied linguistics, as a discipline at the intersection of several academic fields, draws on a variety of theories and perspectives from other related academic disciplines, such as social and educational psychology (Kramsch, 2000). Due to its multidisciplinary ethos, applied linguistics is well positioned to contribute to the scholarship on stereotypes, which is itself a multidisciplinary construct (Nikitina, 2017). I would like to propose that the concept of "system of meaning" introduced in psychology research by Vygotsky (1934) could be fruitfully employed in studies on country stereotypes held by language learners.

Developed and elaborated by Vygotsky (1934), the system of meaning, which incorporates the concepts of "word meaning" (*znachenie slova*) and "word sense" (*smysl*), could provide a suitable theoretical framework for applied linguistics research on mental images held by language learners. To give a gist of these Vygotskian concepts, individual people possess a complex internal system of meaning. This system develops in the course of a person's social interactions with his or her environment, beginning from infancy and continuing throughout life. Though the system of meaning can be conceived as a unity of the thinking and language processes, the concept is, in fact, a rich and multifaceted amalgam of cognitive, intellectual, linguistic, affective and volitional processes. To analyze this complex architectonic, Vygotsky proposed the concept of word meaning (*znachenie slova*) as a primary and irreducible unit of analysis. Clearly, "word" in the Vygotskian network of concepts does not refer solely to a lexical item: it subsumes language as a whole entity.[1]

In the Vygotskian conceptualization, word meaning and word sense form a dyadic unity. As Vygotsky pointed out, word has not only a meaning *znachenie*; word also possesses its own and unique for each individual person sense (*smysl*). While the word meaning is stable and generalizable, which allows intelligible communication among people, it is not static: the meaning develops and shifts over time as a word acquires multiple new layers of associations. Vygotsky argued that this process occurs not only at the level of an individual's cognitive development but also on a wider plane of historical processes that take place within human society. As a result, words inevitably acquire a multitude of psychological associations that are sediments of a multitude of events and experiences associated in our individual and collective consciousness with the world around us and the plethora of its phenomena. The sum of these associations would be embedded in the word sense (*smysl*) which is unique for each individual person.

To extrapolate the theoretical concepts of word meaning (*znachenie slova*) and word sense (*smysl*) for an analysis of language learners' mental images of target language countries, the following sequence of logic could be proposed. The name of a country, which is a stable geographic entity expressed as a lexical item or as a word, has a meaning (*znachenie slova*) that is internalized by individual people, including children and young people, and that is also generalized (or shared) among representatives of a particular national, social or cultural group. The available literature on the development of country stereotypes (Lambert and Klineberg, 1967; Lippmann, 1922/1965; Piaget and Weil, 1951) supports this assumption. Besides the shared word meaning (*znachenie slova*), a country's name expressed as a word (a lexical unit) would evoke a flurry of mental representations and psychological reactions that are endogenous, particular and unique to each individual person. In other words, each individual language learner would endow the name of a target language country with his or her own unique sense (*smysl*) that might not be shared with the other members of a national and social group. This is because each individual person, beginning from infancy, has his or her own unique history of past psychological events, either socially or individually experienced, that are related to the target language country. Interestingly, this line of argumentation can also help to resolve a debate among psychology researchers as to whether stereotypes should be recognized as such only when they are socially shared or whether stereotypes can also be individually held and highly idiosyncratic mental representations.

The current book argues that country stereotypes can be explored as word meaning (*znachenie slova*) that is attached by language learners to the name of a target language country and collectively shared by them. This meaning can be garnered by asking the students to freely recall or *verbalize* mental images they associate with a target language country. This approach also allows for some methodological innovations, such as assessing salience of the country stereotypes. Moreover, Assessing word meaning embedded in the target language country's name is replete with pedagogical implications. This is because, as discussed in Chapter 5, the language classroom allows many affordances for engaging language learners in negotiation, deconstruction and reconstruction of the collective meaning(s) attached to the target language country's name. Such intellectual engagements would be conducive for deepening, expanding, enhancing and enriching the personal sense (*smysl*) that individual learners attach to the country's name.

Note

1 Alex Kozulin's book *Vygotsky's Psychology: A Biography of Ideas* (1990) is an excellent introduction to Lev Vygotsky's intellectual heritage. A concise summary of Vygotsky's theories that are particularly pertinent in the contexts of language teaching and learning can be found in Holbrook Mahn's chapter "Vygotsky and Second Language Acquisition", included in *The Encyclopedia of Applied Linguistics* (2013) edited by Carol A. Chapelle.

References

Ainol, M. Z., & Isarji, H. S. (2009). Motivation to learn a foreign language in Malaysia. *GEMA Online Journal of Language Studies, 9*(2), 73–87.
Aladdin, A. (2010). Non-Muslim Malaysian learners of Arabic (NMMLAs): An investigation of their attitudes and motivation towards learning Arabic as a foreign language in multiethnic and multicultural Malaysia. *Procedia: Social and Behavioral Sciences, 9*, 1805–1811.doi: 10.1016/j.sbspro. 2010.12.404
Attitude. (2013). *Online etymology dictionary*. Retrieved October 1, 2013, from www.etymonline.com/index.php?term=attitude
Bem, D. J. (1970). *Beliefs, attitudes, and human affairs*. Belmont, CA: Brooks/Cole.

Buck, R. (2005). Adding ingredients to the self-organizing dynamic system stew: Motivation,communication, and higher-level emotions—and don't forget the genes! *Behavioral and Brain Science, 28*(2), 197–198.

Busse, V. (2013). An exploration of motivation and self-beliefs of first year students of German. *System, 41*(2), 379–398.

Byon, A. S. (2007). The use of culture portfolio project in a Korean culture classroom: Evaluating stereotypes and enhancing cross-cultural awareness. *Language, Culture and Curriculum, 20*(1), 1–19. doi: 10.2167/lcc323.0

Chaput, P. R. (1997). Culture in grammar. *The Slavic and East European Journal, 41*, 403–414. doi: 10.2307/310183

Csizér, K., & Dörnyei, Z. (2005). The internal structure of language learning motivation and its relationship with language choice and learning effort. *The Modern Language Journal, 89*(1), 19–36. doi: 10.1111/j.0026-7902.2005.00263.x

Csizér, K., & Kormos, J. (2008). The relationship of intercultural contact and language learning motivation among Hungarian students of English and German. *Journal of Multilingual and Multicultural Development, 29*(1), 30–48. doi: 10.2167/jmmd557.0

Csizér, K., & Kormos, J. (2009). Modelling the role of inter-cultural contact in the motivation of learning English as a foreign language. *Applied Linguistics, 30*(2), 166–185. doi: 10.1093/applin/amn025

Dlaska, A. (2000). Integrating culture and language learning in institution-wide language programmes. *Language, Culture and Curriculum, 13*(3), 247–263. doi: 10.1080/07908310008666602

Dörnyei, Z. (2001). *Teaching and researching motivation.* Harlow, Essex: Longman.

Dörnyei, Z. (2005) *The psychology of the language learner: Individual differences in second language acquisition.* Mahwah, NJ: Lawrence Erlbaum.

Dörnyei, Z., & Ryan, S. (2015). *The psychology of the language learner revisited.* Abingdon, UK: Routledge.

Drewelow, I. (2013). Impact of instruction on shaping or reshaping stereotypical cultural representations in an introductory French course. *Foreign Language Annals, 46*(2), 157–174. doi: 10.1111/flan.12029

Eagly, A. H., & Chaiken, S. (1993). *The psychology of attitudes.* Fort Worth, TX: Harcourt, Brace, Jovanovich.

Fishbein, M., & Ajzen, I. (1975). *Belief, attitude, intention and behaviour: An introduction to theory and research.* Reading, MA: Addison-Wesley.

Forbes, C. E., & Schmader, T. (2010). Retraining attitudes and stereotypes to affect motivation and cognitive capacity under stereotype threat. *Journal of Personality and Social Psychology, 99*(5), 740–754. doi: 10.1037/a0020971

Gardner, R. C. (1985). *Social psychology and second language learning: The role of attitudes and motivation.* London: Edward Arnold.

Gardner, R. C. (2010). *Motivation and second language acquisition: The socio-educational model.* New York: Peter Lang Publishing.

Gardner, R. C., & Lambert, W. E. (1959). Motivational variables in second-language acquisition. *Canadian Journal of Psychology/Revue Canadienne de Psychologie, 13*(4), 266–272. doi:10.1037/h0083787

Gardner, R. C., & Lambert, W. E. (1972). *Attitudes and motivation in second-language learning.* Rowley, MA: Newbury House Publishers.

Gearing, N., & Roger, P. (2019). Where's the vision? Rescuing integrativeness to understand the language learning motivation of English-speaking EFL instructors living in South Korea. *System, 82,* 122–131.

Greenwald, A. G., & Banaji, M. R. (1995). Implicit social cognition: Attitudes, self-esteem, and stereotypes. *Psychological Review, 102*(1), 4–27.

Heinzmann, S. (2013). *Young language learners' motivation and attitudes: Longitudinal, comparative and explanatory perspectives.* New York, NY: Bloomsbury.

Higgins, E. T. (1987). Self-discrepancy: A theory relating self and affect. *Psychological Review, 94,* 319–340.

Islam, M., Lamb, M., & Chambers, G. (2013). The L2 motivational self system and national interest: A Pakistani perspective. *System, 41*(2), 231–244.

Kormos, J., Kiddle, T., & Csizér, K. (2011). Systems of goals, attitudes, and self-related beliefs in second-language-learning motivation. *Applied Linguistics, 32*(5), 495–516. doi: 10.1093/applin/amr019

Kozulin, A. (1990). *Vygotsky's psychology: A biography of ideas.* New York: Harvester Wheatsheaf.

Kramsch, C. (2000). Second language acquisition, applied linguistics, and the teaching of foreign languages. *The Modern Language Journal, 84*(3), 311–326.

Lambert, W. E., & Klineberg, O. (1967). *Children's views of foreign people.* New York, NY: Appleton-Century-Crofts.

Lippmann, W. (1922/1965). *Public opinion.* New York, NY: The Free Press.

Mahn, H. (2013). Vygotsky and second language acquisition. In Carol A. Chapelle (Ed.), *The encyclopedia of applied linguistics* (pp. 1–8). John Wiley and Sons Ltd. doi: 10.1002/9781405198431.wbeal1272

Markus, H., & Nurius, P. (1986). Possible selves. *American Psychologist, 41*(9), 954–969.

McGarty, C., Yzerbyt, V. Y., & Spears, R. (2002). *Stereotypes as explanations: The formation of meaningful beliefs about social groups.* Cambridge: Cambridge University Press.

McKenzie, R. M. (2010). *The social psychology of English as a global language: Attitudes, awareness and identity in the Japanese context.* Springer Science & Business Media.

Motivation. (2013). *Online Etymology Dictionary.* Retrieved October 1, 2013, from www.etymonline.com/index.php?allowed_in_frame=0&search=motivation&searchmode=none

Nikitina, L. (2015). Country stereotypes and L2 motivation: A study of French, German and Spanish language learners. *Studies in Linguistics, 37,* 483–509. https://doi.org/10.17002/sil.37.2015010.483

Nikitina, L. (2017). Stereotypes as an interdisciplinary construct: Implications for applied linguistics research. *Suvremena lingvistika, 43*(83), 1–19. https://doi.org/10.22210/suvlin.2017.083.01

Nikitina, L. (2019). Do country stereotypes influence language learning motivation? A study among foreign language learners in Malaysia. *Moderna Språk, 113*(1), 58–79.

Oppenheim, A. N. (1966/2004). *Questionnaire design, interviewing and attitude measurement.* New York: Continuum.

Oskamp, S., & Schultz, P. W. (2005). *Attitudes and opinions* (3rd ed.). Mahwah, NJ: Lawrence Erlbaum Associates.

Piaget, J., & Weil, A. M. (1951). The development in children of the idea of the homeland and of relations with other countries. *International Social Sciences Bulletin: National Stereotypes and International Understanding, 3*(3), 561–578.

Ryan, R. M., & Deci, E. L. (2000). Intrinsic and extrinsic motivations: Classic definitions and new directions. *Contemporary Educational Psychology, 25*(1), 54–67. http://dx.doi.org/10.1006/ceps.1999.1020

Schulz, R., & Haerle, B. M. (1995). "Beer, fast cars, and...": Stereotypes held by U.S. college-level students of German. *Die Unterrichtspraxis/Teaching German, 28*(1), 29–39.

Scott, W. A. (1954/1968). Attitude measurement. In G. Lindzey & E. Aronson (Eds.), *The handbook of social psychology: Historical introduction; systematic positions* (Vol. 2). Reading, MA: Addison-Wesley Publishing Company.

Spencer-Rodgers, J. (2001). Consensual and individual stereotypic beliefs about international students among American host nationals. *International Journal of Intercultural Relations, 25*(6), 639–657. http://dx.doi.org/10.1016/S0147-1767(01)00029-3

Storme, J. A., & Derakhshani, M. (2002). Defining, teaching, evaluating cultural proficiency in the foreign language classroom. *Foreign Language Annals, 35*(6), 657–668.

Tan, T. G., Ooi, A. K., & Hairul, N. I. (2012). The orientations for learning Mandarin amongst Malay undergraduate students. *International Journal of Humanities and Social Science, 2*(12), 104–112.

Taylor, I. C. (1977). Beware of cultural clichés. *Die Unterrichtspraxis/Teaching German, 10*(2), 108–114.

Vygotsky, L. S. (1934). *Myshlenie i rech (Thinking and speech)* (in Russian). Moscow, Leningrad: Gosudarstvennoye Socialno-ekonomicheskoye Izdatel'stvo.

Yang, J. S. R. (2003). Motivational orientations and selected learner variables of East Asian language learners in the United States. *Foreign Language Annals, 36*(1), 44–56. doi: 10.1111/j.1944-9720.2003.tb01931.x

Yu, J., Brown, G. T., & Stephens, J. M. (2018). Retrospective case studies of successful Chinese learners of English: Continuity and change in self-identities over time and across contexts. *System, 72*, 124–138.

3 A mixed-methods approach to link country stereotypes and L2 motivation

The aim of the study, its research questions and research design

This study's aim is two-pronged. Firstly, it seeks to explore stereotypes or mental images of the target languages countries held by learners of six Asian languages – Japanese, Korean, Mandarin, Myanmar, Thai and Vietnamese – in an Asian educational context, such as Malaysia. Secondly, it aspires to demonstrate a comprehensive approach to investigating these stereotypical images and conduct a rigorous systematic analysis of their relationship with L2 motivation. To reflect these aims, the research questions that guided this study were:

1 What consensual stereotypes do the learners of the six Asian languages have of the target language countries?
2 What categories do these mental images form?
3 How favourable and how salient are these categories of images?
4 What are the associations between the language learners' mental images of the target language countries and their L2 motivation?

To find answers to these questions required collecting and analyzing both qualitative (QUAL) and quantitative (QUAN) data and adopting an appropriate research design. Research design is a chain of steps that a researcher takes from the earliest to the last stage of a research project. As Krippendorff (2013) advised, the "research designs should be explicit so that they can be replicated, or critically evaluated for the conclusiveness of the findings" (p. 387). In the current study, a concurrent or parallel mixed methods research design (QUAL+QUAN) was adopted. Figure 3.1 offers a graphical representation of the methodological and analytical flow of this study.

The following section discusses some of the benefits that applied linguistics researchers can garner from adopting mixed methods approaches for an analysis of stereotypes or mental images held by language learners.

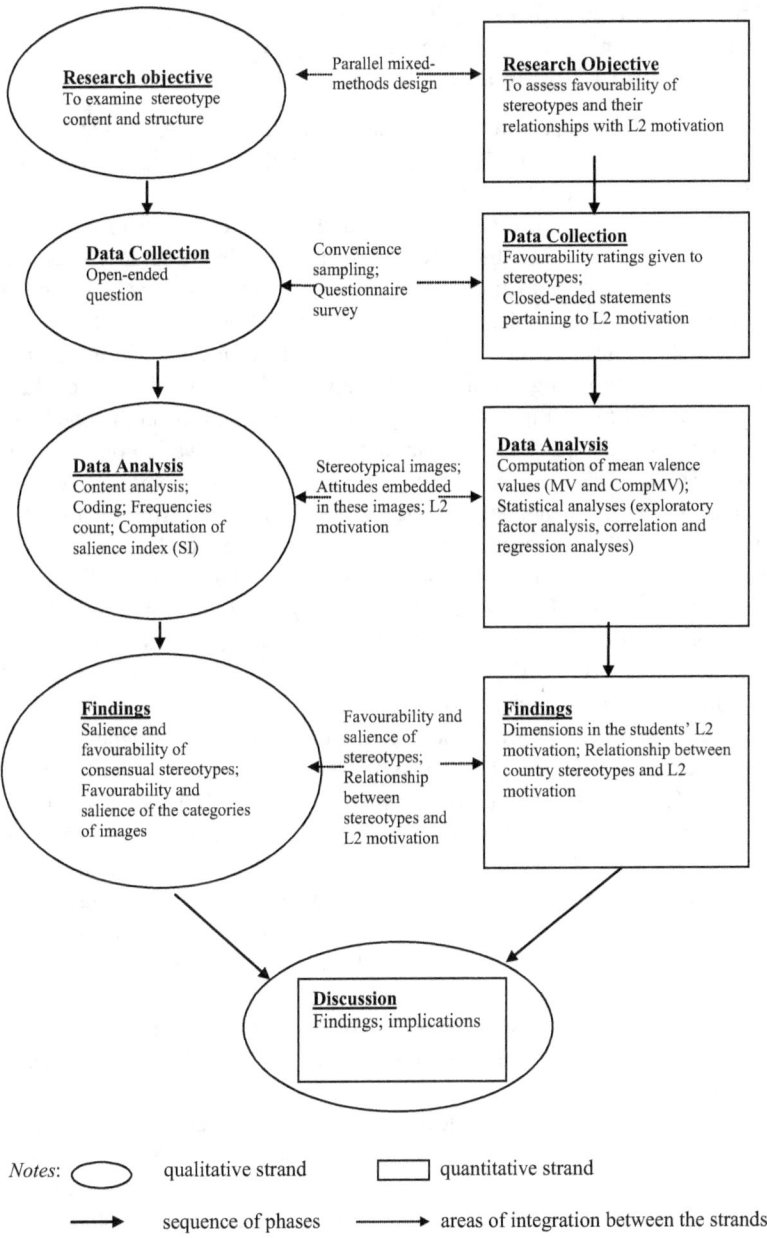

Figure 3.1 Strands and steps in the research design

The need for mixed-methods approaches in research on country stereotypes, language attitudes and L2 motivation

Applied linguistics researchers and language educators agree that mental images or stereotypes that language learners hold about a target language country is an important factor that influences the students' choice of a foreign language to learn (Dlaska, 2000) and their motivation to learn this particular language (Gardner and Lambert, 1972; Nikitina, 2015, 2019). Calls have been made to empirically examine the relationships between the country stereotypes and language learning motivation (Byon, 2007). However, such studies remain scarce. The main reason for this lack of research could be a methodological dissonance between the predominantly qualitative studies of mental images of target language countries on the one hand and the primarily quantitative examinations of L2 motivation on the other hand. To be more specific, the majority of studies that explored country stereotypes held by language learners derived their data from open-ended questions and then proceeded to employ qualitative methods to analyze the data (Allen, 2004; Byon, 2007; Drewelow, 2013; Schulz and Haerle, 1995). In contrast, as Boo, Dörnyei and Ryan (2015) noted, quantitative methods have been dominant in studies on L2 motivation where researchers have traditionally used questionnaires with closed-ended items and employed various statistical procedures to analyze the data.

Much can be gained from adopting mixed-methods approaches in studies on country and national stereotypes, language attitudes and L2 motivation. The obvious benefit is that mixed-methods designs would allow linking the qualitative data on country images with the quantitative data on and assessments of L2 motivation. Collecting and analyzing the numerical or quantitative data pertaining to mental images of target language countries would allow for gaining deeper insights into the nature of country stereotypes, their inner structure and the attitudes embedded in these images. Methodologies for gaining such insights will be introduced in this chapter. Moreover, innovative methodologies would create affordances for adopting interesting theoretical perspectives in research on language learners' country stereotypes.

For example, Vygotskian concepts of a system of meaning, word meaning (*znachenie slova*) and word sense (*smysl*) could serve as propitious theoretical frameworks in applied linguistic studies, especially when the participants are given an opportunity to freely recall their mental images of a target language country and thus are able to express these images in their own words. These words (or lexical entities), besides having a shared generalized word meaning (*znachenie slova*), would reflect more personalized word sense (*smysl*) that each individual student attaches to the country's name. The way the open-ended question was formulated in this study (see the following section) permitted assessing the "meaning" and "sense" that the students attached to the words expressing the target country name, its cultures and people.

The research instrument

This study employed a questionnaire that was specially designed to collect data on the language learners' endogenous images of the target language countries, the attitudes embedded in these images, and the students' L2 motivation. The questionnaire contained one open-ended question, 15 closed-ended items and several questions concerning the students' demographic characteristics (see Appendix 1 for a copy of the questionnaire). The language learners' mental images of the target language countries given as responses to the open-ended question provided the qualitative (QUAL) data. The favourability ratings assigned by the students to the mental images in their individual lists and the answers to the items measuring L2 motivation yielded the quantitative (QUAN) data.

The open-ended question

The open-ended question of the instrument sought to obtain the students' endogenous mental images or stereotypes of the target language country, its cultures, and people; the question was adapted from my own earlier research (Nikitina, 2015, 2019). As an example, the open-ended question posed to the learners of Vietnamese in the current study was "What images or mental pictures come to your mind when you hear the words 'Vietnam' or 'Vietnamese'?". After the students had written their images about the target language country, they were instructed to rate each image in their list on a scale ranging from −2 ("a very negative image") to +2 ("a very positive image").

The closed-ended items to measure L2 motivation

The 15 closed-ended items to measure L2 motivation were adopted from my earlier research on Malaysian language learners' motivation to learn European languages (Nikitina, 2019). This part of the questionnaire assessed the following aspects of the students' L2 motivation:

1 General motivation (items #3, #5, #8, #10, #12 and #13): A high score on this measure corresponded to a high degree of effort and perseverance that a student was willing to expend to learn the target language.

2 Instrumental orientation (items #1, #6, #7, #11 and #14): A high score on this measure suggested that a student assigned a considerable practical utility to the target language (e.g., its usefulness for getting financial benefits, employment or study opportunities).

3 Integrative orientation (items # 2, #4, #9 and #15): A high score on this measure indicated a student's intention to learn the target language for the purpose of communicating with the speakers of this language and having a better understanding of the target language country, its cultures, people and their ways of life.

The respondents marked their answers on 5-point Likert-type scales ranging from −2 ("strongly disagree") to +2 ("strongly agree").

Sampling method and the participants

This study employed a convenience sampling method which is "the most common sample type in L2 research" (Dörnyei, 2007, p. 98) and in studies in the fields of psychology and behavioural sciences (Whitley and Kite, 2013). However, it should be noted that "convenience samples are rarely completely convenience-based but are usually partially purposeful" (Dörnyei, 2007, p. 99). This is definitely the case with the current study where selection of the participants was guided by the following considerations: firstly, they must be undergraduate students at the University of Malaya; secondly, they must be learning one of the Asian – as opposed to European – languages offered in the university.

Non-probabilistic sampling techniques, such as the purposive sampling employed in this study, restrict a researcher's ability to generalize the findings of his or her study to a wider population. In this connection, it should be noted that generalizability of the statistical results was not among the main objectives of this study. The present research endeavours to, firstly, initiate rigorous and systematic explorations of mental images that learners of Asian languages hold about target language countries, their cultures and people. Secondly, it aims to demonstrate how the findings on the contents of the students' country stereotypes, and attitudes embedded in these images, can be linked to empirical assessments of the language learners' L2 motivation.

The participants in this study were 130 (N=130) undergraduate students learning one of the Asian languages offered as an elective course at the University of Malaya. These Asian languages included Mandarin (n=31 or 15.7%), Japanese (n=22 or 11.1%), Korean (n=24 or 12.1%), Thai (n=22 or 11.1%), Myanmar (n=18 or 9.1%) and Vietnamese (n=13 or 6.6%). Among the respondents, 108 students (83.1%) were female and 22 (16.9%) were male, which exceeded the 1:1.6 ratio of male to female students in Malaysian public universities (Ministry of Education Malaysia, 2018).

A mixed-methods approach 45

The age of the respondents was between 20 and 25 years old (Mean=21.72, SD=1.37). All students were majoring in non-science disciplines, namely, linguistics and international relations, and the majority of them (n=90 or 69.2%) were in the first or second year of their university programs. All of the respondents were Malaysian citizens.

Data collection and organization

Data for this study were collected in the years 2018 and 2019, during the foreign language classes attended by the respondents. Prior to the data collection, a permission from the language instructors who were teaching the classes was sought and obtained. Each student was given a photocopied form of the questionnaire. The students were informed about the purpose of the study and reminded that their participation was voluntary: returning the filled-in questionnaire to the researcher implied their consent to participate in this study. The students seemed keen to take part in the survey, and all of them returned the fully answered questionnaires. It took between 15 to 20 minutes for the respondents to complete the questionnaire.

To organize the data, first of all, each questionnaire form collected from the participants was given an identification number. Then, I prepared a separate Microsoft Word file to store the data on each country; in this file I typed *ad verbatim* all mental images provided by each student alongside a unique identification number given to each questionnaire form. The ratings or marks given by the students to their images were typed next to each image. In order to perform a computer-assisted analysis of the mental images using the ANTHROPAC 4.0 software (Borgatti, 1996), the qualitative data – the country images written by the students – were "cleaned". This step involved correcting and unifying the spelling. For example, the spelling of the responses "Jpop", "J-pop" and "j-pop" was unified as "J-pop". Also, the images written in Malay (e.g., *makanan*, which means "food") were translated into English. The quantitative data on L2 motivation and information about the respondents' demographic characteristics were saved as a Microsoft Excel file.

Analysis of the qualitative data

The content analysis

A content analysis was performed to analyze the qualitative data on mental images of the target language countries provided by the students. There are two varieties of content analysis: qualitative and quantitative (Krippendorff, 2013). The former involves a close scrutiny of textual data, organizing the data into analytical categories, and producing a scholarly narrative about the findings. In other words, qualitative content analysis does not rely on numbers. In contrast, quantitative content analysis requires "counting coded textual matter" (Krippendorff, 2013, p. 385) or subjecting it to other quantitative measurements. Importantly, it should be noted that because assigning of the codes to be measured (e.g., categories or labels) is still based on the researcher's subjective judgment, the distinction between the two types of content analyses is largely "one of emphasis" (Krippendorff, 2013, p. 385). In this book, both types of content analysis were performed. The qualitative content analysis established the coding for the students' mental images and organized these images into groups, be it the consensual stereotypes or the bigger categories of images. The quantitative content analysis involved assessing the mental images' frequency, computing the groups' favourability (or valence) and assessing their salience index. As reflected in Figure 3.1.

A qualitative content analysis can be carried out at several levels, such as words, ideological statements, concepts, themes, subject topics and so on (Berg, 2001). In this study, the content analysis was carried out at the level of individual free-lists where the students' mental images of the target language countries were expressed as words and short phrases. The mental images were the unit of analysis or the "information-bearing" instances which cannot be divided further during the analytical procedure (Krippendorff, 2013, p. 98). Importantly, this approach allowed for a seamless linkage between the qualitative (QUAL) and quantitative (QUAN) strands of the analysis. This is because each unit of analysis in the qualitative strand was not only supplied in a free-response manner but also had a numerical rating attached to it by the respondents.

Next, in order to determine the number of times each image had been mentioned, I performed the frequency analysis. This step allowed me to identify consensual stereotypes of the target language countries or the images mentioned by two and more respondents. It is important to note here that, firstly, a distinction was made between the number of *images* and the number of *response items*. Hence, the number of *images* pertaining to each target language country was not equal to the total number of *responses* written by the students. For example, four students mentioned "Bangkok" in their lists of images of Thailand. This means that as a *response item,* "Bangkok" was mentioned four times ($n=4$). However, since it referred to *the same image* – Bangkok, the capital of Thailand – this response item was counted as one ($n=1$) image. Secondly, to be considered a consensual stereotype, an image had to be expressed as either exactly the same lexical item (e.g., "food") or with only minor grammatical or lexical variations (e.g., "festival", "festivals" and "various festivals" formed the consensual stereotype "festivals").

A mixed-methods approach 47

The coding process

In order to have a larger canvas of the students' mental imagery, mental images of each target language country were grouped into larger categories based on the images' similarities. An open-coding approach was adopted in this step of the analysis. This means that the data, rather than a priori established frameworks and themes, determined the codes given to the categories of images (Mackey and Gass, 2005). This analysis did not aim to produce a larger number of homogenous categories of images. This is because the findings about the consensual stereotypes would have already given the readers a good idea as to which images about each target language country were particularly prominent or salient. Therefore, the content analysis aimed to distinguish larger but coherent groups of images.

It must be explicitly acknowledged that any qualitative data analysis would by necessity involve making personal judgments and having "hunches" on the part of a researcher (Ryan and Bernard, 2003, p. 94). It is important, however, to rely on a consistent logic during the decision-making process to ensure that the analysis and the findings are consistent and coherent. After some trial and error, I established a logic model for organizing the country images into larger categories, which was especially useful in the cases when an image could be placed in more than one of the overlapping categories. For example, I decided to place the references to famous personalities and prominent individuals into the category "People" rather than assigning these images to the categories related to the sphere of these individuals' activity, such as popular culture, sports or politics. To give an example, the image "Kang Daniel" (a popular South Korean singer) was placed in the category of images labelled "People", and not in the category named "K-pop, K-drama and entertainment".

In the cases when making a decision was particularly difficult, I consulted the original students' questionnaires in order to get the "feel" of the data and insights into the respondents' thinking process. This helped to determine an appropriate classification for some of the images. For example, the image "cultivation of wasabi" provided by a learner of Japanese was quite difficult to classify. When checking the student's original questionnaire, I found out that this image was preceded and succeeded by various culture-related images of Japan. This suggested that combining the image "cultivation of wasabi" with other culture-related images would yield a more accurate structure of the student's mental representations of Japan. Therefore, I placed this image in the category "Traditional culture and culture symbols".

There were several idiosyncratic images that could not form a coherent category with the other images of a target language country; such images were placed in the category labelled "Others". Since this group combined highly

48 *A mixed-methods approach*

heterogeneous images that did not form a unified whole among themselves, the salience and favourability parameters of the category "Others" were not assessed. However, these images were included when calculating the total number of images. Also, the favourability ratings given by the students to these images were included in the assessments of the overall favourability or composite mean valence (CompMV) of the images.

To establish the reliability of the content analysis, I performed an intracoder reliability check (Van den Hoonaard, 2008). In other words, several weeks after the content analysis was completed, I re-coded a portion of the data for each country. Then, I calculated the intra-rater reliability rate, which is a simple percentage agreement between the coding done at two points in time. In some instances, especially for the data on Japan, I discovered that the agreement rate was about 60%, which is below the desirable percentage agreement of 80–90% recommended by Loewen and Plonsky (2015). Therefore, I reanalyzed the data and performed the intra-rater reliability check again. After the second round of the analysis, the achieved reliability rate was above 80%.

The assessments of stereotype salience and accuracy

Salience refers to a quality of being important, noticeable, prominent and familiar. The analysis of salience was performed on the consensual stereotypes and also on the larger categories of images. The computer software ANTHROPAC 4.0 (Borgatti, 1996) used for this purpose yields the Modified Free-list Salience Index which was developed by Smith, Furbee, Maynard, Quick and Ross (1995). The index can have any value between 0 and 1, and values closer to 1 indicate a higher salience.

Stereotype accuracy was assessed for consensual stereotypes of the target language countries. The "common–unique" continuum developed by Echtner and Ritchie (1993) was used as a heuristic device. Stereotypes that referred to specific sites and phenomena to be found in or originating from a particular target language country (e.g., "Beijing" in China, "Muay Thai" in the list of images of Thailand) were considered as "unique". The number of these images in the total number of consensual stereotypes allowed for making conclusions about the accuracy of language learners' mental imagery of the target language country.

Analysis of the quantitative data

The quantitative data in this study were obtained from the favourability or valence ratings (ranging from −2 to +2) that the students had assigned to each item in their lists of images, and also from the students' answers to the 15 questionnaire statements pertaining to their L2 motivation. The analysis of the quantitative data involved, firstly, the assessment of favourability or valence[1] of consensual stereotypes and larger categories of images, and, secondly, the statistical analysis of the relationship between the language learners' mental images and their L2 motivation (see Figure 3.1).

The statistical tests included the exploratory factor analysis (EFA), correlation and regression analyses (see Figure 3.1). The following sections give a detailed explanation of the analytical procedure.

The calculation of mean valence (MV)

The assessment of the mental images' valence or favourability included, firstly, calculating the mean valence (MV) of consensual stereotypes and of larger categories of images. To calculate the MV values, I divided the sum total of the ratings given to all images in a group (e.g., the consensual stereotypes or category of images) by the number of images it contained. This calculation can be expressed in the following mathematical formula which was adopted with some modifications from Spencer-Rodgers (2001):

$$MV_j = \frac{\sum_{i=1}^{F_j} V_{ji}}{F_j}$$

where MV_j is the mean valence of a group of images j; V_{ji} is the valence ratings given to the i-th image in this group j; F_j is the number of images in the group j. The calculations were performed with the aid of the Microsoft Excel program.

The calculation of composite mean valence (CompMV)

Secondly, the computation of overall favourability or composite mean valence (CompMV) of the images of each target language country was done. In other words, I divided the sum total of the ratings given to all images of a target language country by the number of the images.

The formula used for the calculations was adopted with some modifications from Spencer-Rodgers (2001):

$$CompMV = \frac{\sum_{i=1}^{M} V_i}{M}$$

where V_i is the valence ratings given to the i-th image of a target language country, and M is the total number of images of this particular country. The calculations were done using the Microsoft Excel program.

The statistical analysis

The assessment of the relationship between the students' mental images of a target language country and their L2 motivation included the correlation and regression analyses. Prior to these statistical tests, I performed an exploratory factor analysis (EFA), which is explained in the following section.

Ultimately, the statistical analyses helped to establish whether the students' attitudes embedded in the mental images of target language countries, which were measured by the favourability ratings, would correlate with their L2 motivation, which was assessed through their answers to the closed-ended items of the questionnaire. The IBM SPSS Statistics V25.0 computer software was used to perform the statistical tests. Figure 3.2 gives a visual representation of the chronological order of the statistical analyses.

A more detailed explanation of the statistical procedures and rationales behind their application is given in the following sections.

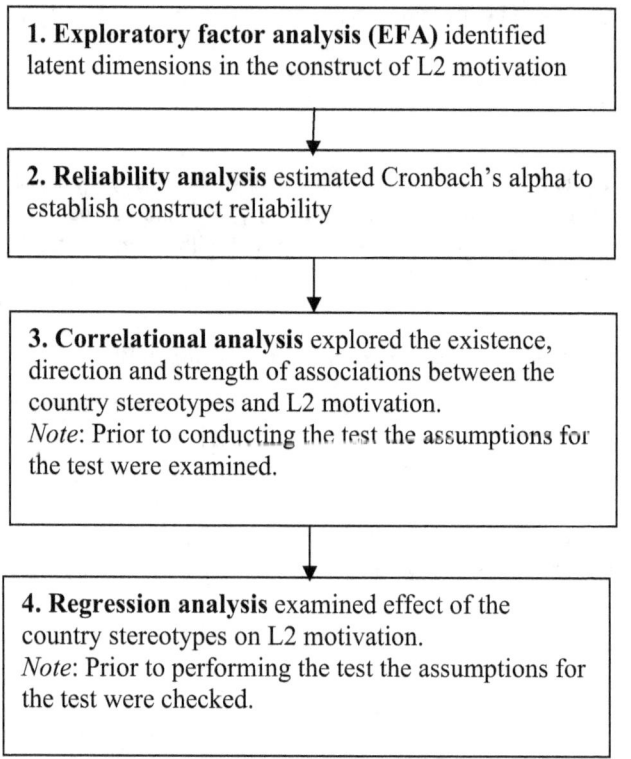

Figure 3.2 Sequence of the quantitative analysis

The analysis of L2 motivation: exploratory factor analysis (EFA)

Factor analysis is performed by researchers in order "to define the underlying structure among the variables in the analysis" (Hair, Black, Babin, Anderson and Tatham, 2006, p. 104). The exploratory factor analysis (EFA) determines the sets of interrelated variables – known as "factors" – among all the variables submitted to the analysis. These factors represent the dimensions or constructs within the dataset. In the current study, the EFA helped to identify the underlying structure or dimensions in the construct of L2 motivation. The EFA analysis was performed using the principal component model and the varimax rotation method with Kaiser normalization. According to Hair et al. (2006), the varimax rotation method, of which the Kaiser normalization procedure is a part, gives "a clearer separation of the factors" (p. 126).

It is important to note that the factors produced by EFA are "extracted from the data". In other words, they are derived from the dataset and may not entirely align with variables included in a theory adopted by a researcher (Hair et al., 2006). Also, the composition of the items that a factor has loaded may – and, most probably, will – vary among research studies. For these reasons, it is advisable that applied linguistics researchers always subject their dataset to the EFA first and then only proceed to perform the ensuing statistical tests using the variables obtained through the EFA.

The reliability analysis: Cronbach's alpha

In order to establish reliability of the construct of L2 motivation, the Cronbach's alpha (α) was computed in the following step of the analysis. Reliability is the "extent to which a variable or set of variables is consistent in what it is intended to measure" (Hair et al., 2006, p. 103). Acceptable values of the Cronbach's α is a much-debated issue. However, as methodological literature suggests, an "acceptable" Cronbach's α would depend on the academic field and nature of a study. According to Nunnally (1967), in studies of a theoretical nature, modest reliabilities of .60 or .50 may be acceptable. In psychological research, Cronbach's α of .60 or even lower can be considered adequate; however, the desired values would be expected to exceed .70 (Aron and Aron, 1999, p. 527). To concur, Hair et al. (2006) maintain that "the generally agreed upon lower limit for Cronbach's alpha is .70 although it may decrease to .60" (p. 137). In applied linguistics research, it is suggested that the Cronbach's α reliability coefficients should preferably exceed .70, but the .60 value could be an acceptable lower limit (Dörnyei, 2007).

A mixed-methods approach

The correlation analysis: Spearman correlation test

Correlation analysis is concerned with the associations or connections between the variables (Huck, 2012). The current study examined associations between the language learners' mental images of a target language country and their L2 motivation. Prior to conducting the correlation analysis, I checked the assumptions for the appropriateness of this procedure. The data was found to be non-normal, and there were several outliers in the dataset. Therefore, the non-parametric Spearman correlation test was performed. In this statistical procedure, the correlation coefficient or Spearman's rho (r_s) indicates the strengths and direction of the associations. The value of the r_s ranges between −1 and +1, and the correlation coefficient that is close to either end of the range shows a stronger association. The signs "+" and "−" show the direction of the association which can be either "direct" (indicated by the "+" sign) or "inverse' (signalled by the "−" sign). The 0 value indicates the absence of an association between the variables (Hair et al., 2006).

As to what constitutes the size of the correlation coefficient, the answer would depend on the academic discipline. For research that deals with psychological constructs, Cohen (1977) considers a correlation of .10 as "small", of .30 as "medium" and of .50 and above as "large" (pp. 78–80). Aron and Aron (1999) noted that "it is rare to obtain correlations that are greater than .40" (p. 89) in the behavioural sciences research.

The regression analysis

Multiple regression analyses were performed in the following step. The results helped to establish the magnitude of the country stereotypes' effect on the students' L2 motivation. A robust method was employed to estimate the regression coefficients (see Nikitina, Paidi and Furuoka, 2019). This means that the confidence intervals (CI) rather than *p*-values were computed and reported. Since the SPSS 25 software versions used in this study did not allow for performing the robust regression statistical procedure, special codes were written to enable such an analysis. These codes are available in Appendix 3.[2]

Notes

1 Regarding the terminology, the terms "valence" and "favourability" are used interchangeably in this book in order to avoid the oxymoron expression "negative favourability". "Valence" is a more encompassing term because it incorporates the "direction" of an attitude which can be positive, negative or neutral (Maio and Haddock, 2010, p. 4).
2 I would like to thank Fumitaka Furuoka for writing the codes.

References

Allen, L. Q. (2004). Implementing a culture portfolio project within a constructivist paradigm. *Foreign Language Annals*, *37*(2), 232–239. doi: 10.1111/j.1944-9720.2004.tb02196.x

Aron, A., & Aron, E. (1999). *Statistics for psychology* (2nd ed.). Upper Saddle River, NJ: Prentice Hall.

Berg, B. L. (2001). *Qualitative research methods for the social sciences*. Needham Heights, MA: Pearson and Allyn & Bacon.

Boo, Z., Dörnyei, Z., & Ryan, S. (2015). L2 motivation research 2005–2014: Understanding a publication surge and a changing landscape. *System*, *55*, 145–157. https://doi.org/10.1016/j.system.2015.10.006

Borgatti, S. P. (1996). *ANTHROPAC 4.0*. Natick, MA: Analytic Technologies.

Byon, A. S. (2007). The use of culture portfolio project in a Korean culture classroom: Evaluating stereotypes and enhancing cross-cultural awareness. *Language, Culture and Curriculum*, *20*(1), 1–19. doi: 10.2167/lcc323.0

Cohen, J. (1977). *Statistical power analysis for the behavioral sciences*. Hillsdale, NJ: Lawrence Erlbaum Associates, Inc.

Dlaska, A. (2000). Integrating culture and language learning in institution-wide language programmes. *Language, Culture and Curriculum*, *13*(3), 247–263. doi: 10.1080/07908310008666602

Dörnyei, Z. (2007). *Research methods in applied linguistics: Quantitative, qualitative and mixed methodologies*. Oxford: Oxford University Press.

Drewelow, I. (2013). Impact of instruction on shaping or reshaping stereotypical cultural representations in an introductory French course. *Foreign Language Annals*, *46*(2), 157–174. doi: 10.1111/flan.12029

Echtner, C. M., & Ritchie, J. R. B. (1993). The measurement of destination image: An empirical assessment. *Journal of Travel Research*, *31*(4), 3–13.

Gardner, R. C., & Lambert, W. E. (1972). *Attitudes and motivation in second-language learning*. Rowley, MA: Newbury House Publishers.

Hair, J. F., Black, W. C., Babin, B. J., Anderson, R. E., & Tatham, R. L. (2006). *Multivariate data analysis*. Prentice Hall Pearson Education.

Huck, S. W. (2012). *Reading statistics and research* (6th ed.). Pearson.

Krippendorff, K. (2013). *Content analysis: An introduction to its methodology* (3rd ed.). Thousand Oaks, CA: Sage Publications.

Loewen, S., & Plonsky, L. (2015). *An A–Z of applied linguistics research methods*. Macmillan International Higher Education.

Mackey, A., & Gass, S. M. (2005). *Second language research: Methodology and design*. Mahwah, NJ: Lawrence Erlbaum Associates.

Maio, G. R., & Haddock, G. (2010). *The psychology of attitudes and attitude change*. London: Sage Publications.

Ministry of Education Malaysia (2018). *Quick facts 2018: Malaysia educational statistics*. Putrajaya. Available online from https://www.moe.gov.my/penerbitan/1587-quick-facts-2018-malaysia-educational-statistics-1/file

Nikitina, L. (2015). Country stereotypes and L2 motivation: A study of French, German and Spanish language learners. *Studies in Linguistics*, *37*, 483–509. https://doi.org/10.17002/sil.37.2015010.483

Nikitina, L. (2019). Do country stereotypes influence language learning motivation? A study among foreign language learners in Malaysia. *Moderna Språk*, *113*(1), 58–79. Retrieved from http://ojs.ub.gu.se/ojs/index.php/modernasprak/article/view/4675

Nikitina, L., Paidi, R., & Furuoka, F. (2019). Using bootstrapped quantile regression analysis for small sample research in applied linguistics: Some methodological considerations. *PLoS One*, *14*(1), e0210668. https://doi.org/10.1371/journal.pone.0210668

Nunnally, J. C. (1967). *Psychometric theory*. New York: McGraw-Hill.

Ryan, G. W., & Bernard, H. R. (2003). Techniques to identify themes. *Field Methods*, *15*(1), 85–109.

Schulz, R. A., & Haerle, B. M. (1995). "Beer, fast cars, and...": Stereotypes held by U.S. college-level students of German. *Die Unterrichtspraxis/Teaching German*, *28*(1), 29–39. Retrieved from www.jstor.org/stable/3531331?seq=1#metadata_info_tab_contents

Smith, J. J., Furbee, L., Maynard, K., Quick, S., & Ross, L. (1995). Salience counts: A domain analysis of English color terms. *Journal of Linguistic Anthropology*, *5*(2), 203–216. Retrieved from www.jstor.org/stable/43103137?seq=1

Spencer-Rodgers, J. (2001). Consensual and individual stereotypic beliefs about international students among American host nationals. *International Journal of Intercultural Relations*, *25*(6), 639–657. http://dx.doi.org/10.1016/S0147-1767(01)00029-3

Van den Hoonaard, W. C. (2008). Inter-and intracoder reliability. In L. M. Given (Ed.), *The Sage encyclopedia of qualitative research methods* (pp. 445–446). Thousand Oaks, CA: Sage Publications.

Whitley, B. E., & Kite, M. E. (2013). *Principles of research in behavioral science* (3rd ed.). New York, NY: Routledge.

4 Findings on language learners' country stereotypes and their relationships with L2 motivation

Language learners' mental images of the target language countries

Language learners' mental images of China

A total of 161 (N=161) mental images of China were provided by 31 learners of Mandarin in this study. The two longest lists of images contained 18 items each, while the three shortest inventories had only 2 images. On average, each student generated 6 images per list and the mode number was 6.

Consensual stereotypes of China

Among the 161 mental representations of China, 30 images were mentioned by two or more students and, hence, these images formed consensual stereotypes of the target language country (see Table A4.1 in Appendix 2). The highly salient images that tended to appear at the top of the students' lists were "(China has) many people" (n=8; SI=0.228; SR=1), "big country" (n=6; SI=0.218; SR=2), "culture" (n=4; SI=0.153; SR=3), "delicious food" (n=6; SI=0.13; SR=4), "communism" (n=4; SI=0.129; SR=5), and "technology" (n=7; SI=0.122; SR=6). Interestingly, two of the most salient consensual stereotypes – "many people" and "communism" – had negative mean valence values. This means that the students tended to assign predominantly negative marks (−1 or −2) to these images. The other images that had a negative valence but were less prominent, as reflected in their salience parameters, were "unfriendly" (n=2; MV=−1.00; SI=0.05; SR=13), "selfish" (n=2; MV=−1.50; SI=0.021; SR=29) and "a difficult to learn language" (n=2; MV=−0.33; SI=0.016; SR=30).

Despite the presence of some negative images, for the most part the consensual stereotypes of China were positive, and they represented various country-related aspects, including China's millennia-long history and rich culture (e.g., "5000 years of history", "Chinese literature", "poetry") and its status as a modern rapidly developing country (e.g., "fast paced country", "modern country", "economy", "developed country"). Some students perceived China as a "mystery", "complex" and a "strong country"; among the perceived qualities of Chinese people were mentioned "hardworking", "smart", "patriotic" and, somewhat less flattering, "selfish" and "unfriendly". There were also references to the capital city of Beijing and the Great Wall, several consensual stereotypes pertained to President of the People's Republic of China Xi Jinping. Other mental images that formed consensual stereotypes were "tea" and "Weibo" (a Chinese microblogging site). As to stereotype accuracy, mostly, the students' mental images of China were not concrete. Only four of the 30 consensual stereotypes pertained specifically to China (i.e., "Beijing", "Xi Jinping", "Great Wall" and "Weibo") while an additional two images – "5000 years of history" and "Chinese literature" – could be placed quite close to the "unique" end of the "common–unique" continuum. The remaining 24 consensual stereotypes could pertain to other countries and were not exclusive to China.

Categories of images of China

In the following step of the analysis, all mental images of China provided by the students, including those that did not form the consensual stereotypes, were classified into categories and assigned a label based on the unifying theme for these images (see Table A4.2 in Appendix 2). Fifteen categories were formed, not including the category "Others". Following this, favourability or mean valence and salience of each category was calculated. The category with the highest favourability value was "Mysterious and complex country" (MV=1.75; MVR=1). It included the images "mystery", "complex" and "mysterious country". However, it was the smallest and the least salient category of images (SI=0.078; SR=13). Closely following in the favourability parameter was the category "Cuisine and food" (MV=1.70; MVR=2). It contained the references to "cuisine" and "Chinese food". Some students mentioned that China has "a lot of delicious food" and that "each area had its own cuisine", while other respondents gave less eloquent answers, such as "tea" or "food". One student mentioned "xiaolongbao", which is a type of steamed bun. The majority of the images in the category "Cuisine and food" were rated +2, which contributed to a high favourability of this category. By salience, the category "Cuisine and food" occupied a middle position (SI=0.132; SR=9). The next in the favourability cluster was "Literature and poetry" (MV=1.60; MVR=3); it contained the images "Chinese literature", "poems", "poetry" and "books". All images in this category received positive ratings +2 and +1. However, as the low salience (SI=0.049; SR=14) of

Language learners' country stereotypes   57

this cluster suggests, the images pertaining to Chinese literature and poetry tended to come to the students' minds as an afterthought and were placed in the end of the students' lists.

Reflecting China's recent technological advancements, some students provided the images "technology", "high tech", "good technology" and "the best technology in the world". These images formed the category "Technology" (MV=1.57; MVR=4). All but two images in this category were given the highest possible rating, +2. Despite a high favourability, the category had a low salience (SI=0.122; SR=11). It was the opposite case with the category "Traditional culture and culture symbols", which not only enjoyed high favourability (MV=1.40; MVR=5) but was also the second most salient group of images of China (SI=0.245; SR=2). In other words, the students' rather frequent references to China's cultural heritage were placed at the top of their lists. These images included "calligraphy", "traditional culture", "classical culture", "traditional clothes", "Chinese New Year", "red colour" and "dragon". Only one student assigned a neutral rating to the image "traditional culture"; the rest of the responses were given the marks +1 and +2. The next in favourability category was named "Social media and e-commerce" (MV=1.25; MVR=6). It contained references to China's prominent status as a cyberspace entity. Besides the images "social media" and "e-commerce", this category included references to China's messaging and mobile payment app "WeChat", the online shopping website "Taobao", the online paying platform "Alipay" and the internet service provider "QQ". All of these images were positively evaluated by the students, except for "e-commerce", which was rated 0. Notwithstanding their high favourability, these images did not appear at the top of the students' lists, as reflected in a low salience of this category (SR=0.038; SI=15).

The category "History" (MV=1.22; MVR=7) was among the top three most salient clusters of images of China (SI=0.233; SR=3). The responses placed in this category acknowledged China's long and complex history (e.g., "5000 years of history", "ancient" and "complex history"). One of the images was "Sina", the word that derives from the Sanskrit word for China. The images in this category were predominantly positive; only two students gave the neutral rating 0 to the representations, "history" and "5000 years of history". Besides acknowledging China's rich traditional culture and its long history, some students described China as a modern "developed country" and "advanced country", while others made references to "business" and "economy". These images formed the category "Advanced and developed country". One student wrote that China's economy "has developed drastically in recent years" and another laconically stated "economic miracle". As reflected in the favourability parameters, this category occupied a middle position in favourability (MV=1.10; MVR=8). The majority of the students assigned the ratings +2 and +1 to the responses placed in this cluster, though there were several neutrally rated images (e.g., "advanced country", "developed country" and "economic miracle"). As to the salience measures, the category occupied a rather high place (SI=0.152; SR=6), which means that the students tended to rapidly recall these images.

Among the categories of images of China, several had the mean valence values below 1.00. These categories were "Cities, places and sites" (MV=0.90; MVR=9), "Modern, fast paced and strong country" (MV=0.71; MVR=10), "Big country" (MV=0.71; MVR=10), "Language" (MV=0.67; MVR=11) and "People" (MV=0.32; MVR=13). To be more specific, the category "Cities, places and sites" contained references to China's capital city, Beijing, to the city of Shanghai, to Jianghan District located in Hubei Province and to the special administrative region of Hong Kong. Some students mentioned the Great Wall of China, one student provided the image "mainland China", while another respondent wrote "Taiwan". It should be noted that the students assigned negative ratings to the images "Taiwan" and "Hong Kong". The image "mainland China" was rated as neutral, while the other images in this cluster were given the positive marks +2 and +1. This category had a low salience (SI=0.113; SR=12), which indicates that the images it contained tended to appear near the end of the students' lists.

The category "Modern, fast paced and strong country" was comprised of the images "modern country", "strong country", "fast paced", "lively country" and "mighty". In this category, the image "mighty" was perceived as negative and given the rating −2. The responses "fast paced" and "lively country" were rated as neutral, while the rest of the images were given positive marks. This category occupied a middle position in salience (SI=0.14; SR=8). Next, the images "big", "huge", "big country" and "the largest country in the world" were mentioned frequently enough to form the category "Big country". While there were no negatively marked images in this group, the highest rating assigned to an image was +1 and not +2. Two students marked their response "big country" as neutral. In view that the mental images of China were collected among learners of Mandarin, it comes as no surprise that some of the mental representations pertained to the target language itself. These images formed the category "Language" (MV=0.67; MVR=11). However, as indicated by the category's comparatively low salience (SI=0.13; SR=10), the language-related images were not among the first mental representations to come to the collective mind of the respondents. In addition, some of the images in this group were given the lowest possible rating −2 (e.g., "Chinese words", "grammatically complex", "difficult to learn language" and "Mandarin"), which resulted in a lower favourability of this group.

The category "People" with its 38 images was the largest and most salient group of mental images of China. This means that the students not only provided a large number of images pertaining to the inhabitants of mainland

China, but they also tended to rapidly retrieve these images from their collective mind. It should be noted that the category "People" had the lowest positive mean valence value (MV=0.32), which reflects somewhat ambivalent attitudes held by the respondents. Some of the perceived character traits and behaviour that the language learners assigned to the mainland Chinese were "arrogant", "close minded", "not friendly", "selfish", "people speak loudly" and "people do not have a good attitude". All of these images were given the negative ratings −1 and −2, which resulted in the category's low favourability. Quite surprisingly, such apparently positive personal qualities as "realistic" and "proud of their country" were also given negative marks. At the same time, the negative perceptions of the Chinese people were quantitatively outweighed by the positive images "clever", "hardworking", "intelligent", "good at maths", "talented", "equipped with knowledge", "successful", "smart" and "innovative". Many of the positively rated images pertained to the perceived physical appearance of mainland Chinese people (e.g., "handsome guys", "pretty girls") and to the people's personal values (e.g., "patriotism"). Some of the images in this category referred to internationally famous people, such as philosopher Confucius, President of the People's Republic of China Xi Jinping, and founder of the Alibaba Group Jack Ma.

There were two categories of images of China that had negative mean valence values – "Large population" (MV=−0.13; MVR=14) and "Political system and international status" (MV=− 0.63; MVR=15). In the former category, only one respondent marked the image "large number of citizens" as positive (+1). The majority of the students gave negative marks to their images "large population", "crowds of people" and "many people"; only a few students marked similar images (e.g., "high population", "China has many people") in their own lists as neutral. Despite its low favourability, the category "Large population" occupied the fourth position in salience (SI=0.228; SR=4). Finally, the least favourable category, "Political system and international status", contained the images "communism", "international" and "a country that will affect the global economy". Interestingly, some students assigned the neutral rating 0 to their image "communism" while others marked it as negative. The responses pertaining to China's international status were marked as neutral. In salience, this category occupied a middle position (SI=0.147; SR=7).

Language learners' mental images of Japan

The 22 learners of Japanese provided 185 (*N*=185) images of the target language country. The longest list of images contained, quite impressively, 41 responses, while the 2 shortest inventories had 4 images each. The average number of images per respondent was 12 and the mode was 5.

Consensual stereotypes of Japan

As stated earlier, the images mentioned by two and more respondents were considered as consensual stereotypes. In total, 38 consensual stereotypes of Japan were identified (see Table A4.3 in Appendix 2). The high number of such images indicates that the language learners had a very rich mental imagery of the target language country. It also should be noted that the consensual stereotypes of Japan in this study include various country-related aspects ranging from the references to Japanese food (e.g., "sushi", "takoyaki", "ramen", "natto" and "wasabi") to cultural traditions (e.g., "tea drinking ceremony"), from the mentions of Japanese traditional attire (e.g., "kimono", "yukata") to casual wear designers and retailers (e.g., "Uniqlo"). Among the consensual stereotypes were the references to popular tourist landmarks, such as Mount Fuji, the electronics shopping hub Akihabara located in central Tokyo, and the capital's major commercial and business area Shibuya. Consensual stereotypes pertaining to Japanese modern culture were "anime", "manga", "cosplay" and "J-pop", while the realities of Japan's contemporary society were represented in the images "ageing society", "discipline", "cleanliness" and "low crime rate". The consensual stereotypes "technology", "Toyota" and "Shinkansen" acknowledged Japan's technological achievements and its international status as a car maker.

The most frequently mentioned consensual stereotypes were "ageing society", "Tokyo", "samurai" and "cleanliness"; each of these mental representations was given by four respondents. The top five most salient consensual stereotypes were "sushi" (SI=0.402; SR=1), "sakura" (SI=0.344; SR=2), "anime" (SI=0.334; SR=3), "kimono" (SI=0.264; SR=4) and "yukata" (SI=0.163; SR=5). In other words, these five images tended to be rapidly retrieved from the respondents' minds and, as a result, placed at the top of their lists. Regarding the consensual stereotypes' favourability, the overwhelming majority of the images were positive. The most favourable stereotypes were "cleanliness", "Akihabara", "Mount Fuji", "summer festival", "Toyota", wasabi", "economy" and "low crime rate". Among the negative consensual stereotypes of Japan were "ageing society", "tsunami" and "nuclear power plant" (which most probably referred to the Fukushima Daiichi Nuclear Power Plant accident in 2011). The analysis of consensual stereotypes also allowed to conclude that the language learners' mental images of Japan were rather accurate. Out of 38 consensual stereotypes of Japan, 27 images referred uniquely to "things Japanese".

Categories of images of Japan

In the next step of the analysis, the 185 mental images of Japan were classified into 15 categories, excluding the category "Others" (see Table A4.4 in Appendix 2). The discussion of the findings will begin with the most favourable categories of images, namely, "Modern lifestyle", "Seasons" and "Economy". All of these groups of images had the highest possible mean valence value (MV=2), which indicates that each and every image in these clusters was given the highest positive rating +2. The category "Modern lifestyle" had the largest number of images (*n*=5). It contained references to Japan's clean and tidy surroundings (e.g., "the cleanest country in the world"), to the ubiquitous presence of the wending machines ("wending machines", "gachapon") and to the low crime rate in the country ("zero crime rate"). Despite the high favourability ratings, these images tended to come to the collective mind of the respondents as an afterthought, which resulted in a low salience of this category (SI=0.127; SR=10). Next, the category labelled "Economy" contained only two images – "economy" and "economic development"; it was the smallest and the least salient group of images of Japan (SI=0.037; SR=15).

The next in favourability was the category "People" (MV=1.89; MVR=4). It contained the images pertaining to the perceived character of Japanese people (e.g., "friendly people", "people are nice", "people are tidy" and "punctual"), their behaviour (e.g., "they cycle while wearing formal attire") and physical appearance (e.g., "cute and beautiful young generation"). Also placed in this category were the references to Prime Minister Shinzo Abe and prominent Buddhist philosopher, practitioner and educator Daisaku Ikeda. One student provided as an image of Japan the name of their language teacher, Azni-sensei. All but one image in the category "People" received the highest rating +2, which resulted in the high favourability of this group of images. As to the salience parameters, the category "People" occupied a middle position in prominence (SI=0.173; SR=7).

One would invariably expect images pertaining to technological advancement and famous car makers to be present in people's mental imagery of Japan. This was the case in the current study. In acknowledgement of Japan's impressive technological achievements, the students provided the references to "high technology", "Shinkansen" and "bullet train". These images and the references to "Honda", "Nissan", "Toyota" and "Mitsubishi", which all refer to the world-famous car brands and car makers, formed the category "Technology and car makers" (MV=1.82; MVR=5). Almost all of these images received the highest possible favourability rating, +2. In addition, this category was among the most voluminous clusters of images of Japan (*n*=11) and had a relatively high salience (SI=0.187; SR=6). Next in favourability was the category "Social values" (MV=1.60; MVR=6). It contained the references to "high moral values", "manners and etiquette", "discipline" and "honne and tatemae". "Honne and tatemae" refers to a cultural phenomenon in Japanese society which pertains to contradictions between an individual person's (often concealed) genuine feelings or opinions (*honne*) and the publicly voiced opinions that confirm to socially endorsed norms (*tatemae*). This mental representation is the only image in the category "Social values" that received the neutral rating 0; the majority of the images were marked +2. It should be noted that this category was among the top five most salient groups of images of Japan (SI=0.202; SR=5). This means that the students tended to recall these images quite rapidly and, as a result, placed them at the top or near the top of their lists of images.

Closely following in favourability was the category "Traditional culture and culture symbols" (MV=1.53; MVR=7); it was the second most salient (SI=0.534; SI=2) category of images of Japan. The category contained references to traditional arts (e.g., "kabuki", "theatre arts"), ritualized practices (e.g., "tea ceremony"), customs (e.g., "bon odori"), festivals (e.g., "summer festival", "tanabata matsuri", "festival – matsuri"), religious practices and symbols (e.g., "Shinto", "shrines") and traditional attire (e.g., "kimono" and "yukata"). The images "geisha" (referring to professional female entertainers highly skilled in traditional Japanese arts, dance and music) and "ninja" (referring to a spy, mercenary or hitman in feudal Japan) were also placed in this category. It should be noted that the images "geisha" and "ninja" have become staple stereotypes of Japan and ubiquitous features in Japanese and international pop culture. The majority of images in the category "Traditional culture and culture symbols" were rated +2 by the respondents. There were no images with the negative ratings and only two images ("geisha" and "theatre arts") were rated as neutral. Next, the group of images named "Cities, places and sites" (MV=1.53; MVR=7) had the same favourability parameters but a slightly lower salience (SI=0.285; SR=4). This category contained references to Japan's capital city, Tokyo, and its famous landmarks Tokyo Tower and Shibuya Street, which the respondent described as "the busiest street in the world". Also included in this cluster was the image "Harajuku", which is famous for its youth culture district in Tokyo. Another Tokyo landmark placed in this category was the shopping hub Akihabara. Among the images pertaining to various cities and places were Kyoto, Osaka, Mount Fuji and Okayama prefecture. The overwhelming majority of images in the category "Cities, places and sites" were given positive marks; only one respondent gave the neutral rating 0 to the image "Tokyo".

The category "Food and beverages" (MV=1.33; MVR=9) was the most voluminous and salient (SI=0.541; SR=1) category of images of Japan. This finding suggests that the students were not only well familiar with Japanese cuisine but also tended to rapidly recall food-related images from their memory. Sushi, the "international staple" of Japanese cuisine, was the most frequently given image. It was followed by a popular snack, "takoyaki" (fried flour balls filled with minced octopus and other condiments), a delicacy of thinly sliced fresh raw fish, "sashimi", and the noodle dishes "ramen", "udon" and "soba". Some students mentioned "natto" (fermented soya beans), "wasabi" (Japanese horseradish and a mustard-like condiment) and "seaweeds", while others recalled traditional Japanese desserts and sweets (i.e., "kakigori" and "daifuku"). Among the beverages, the students mentioned "green tea", "Asahi beer" and the soft drink "Calpis". The majority of images in this category were rated positively; only two students gave the negative rating −1 to the images "natto" and "sashimi". Next, references to the brands originating from Japan formed the category "Brands" (MV=1.13; MVR=10); it contained the images "Uniqlo", "Daiso", "Lawson" (the franchise chains) and "G-shock" (the watch brand). The students gave predominantly positive ratings to these images. Despite the positive attitudes, these images were not placed at the top of the students' lists, which resulted in a low salience of this cluster (SI=0.099; SR=12) of this category.

Some categories of images of Japan had a comparatively low favourability, as their mean valence values were below 1. These categories were "Language" (MV=0.78; MVR=11), "Pop culture" (MV=0.43; MVR=12) and "History" (MV=0.20; MVR=13). The group of images labelled "Language" contained references to the Japanese writing system (i.e., "katakana", "hiragana" and "kanji"). One student simply stated "Japanese language", while another provided the image "Japanglish" (an umbrella term for the varieties of "mixtures" of Japanese and English languages). One of the images placed in this category – "makudonarudo" (meaning "McDonald's") – is an example of Japanglish. The majority of images in the category "Language" were rated positively (+2 and +1); only two students marked the "Japanese language" and the "kanji" responses as very negative (−2). These low marks affected the overall favourability of this category. In salience, the category "Language" occupied a middle position (SI=0.153; SR=8). Next, the category "Pop culture", despite its lower favourability, was one of the most voluminous groups of images of Japan. In this category, "anime" and "manga" were the dominant responses; also, the category contained many references to anime and manga characters, such as "Totoro", "Naruto", "Robot Gundam" and "Shinso". One student mentioned "hentai" (a sexually explicit subgenre of manga and anime). Other images placed in this category were "J-pop", "karaoke", "Arashi" (a Japanese boy band), *Super Sentai* (a TV series) and *Tokyo Drift* (a movie). Two students came up with the image "cosplay" (an abbreviation for "costume play") which refers to a popular culture phenomenon where the participants wear costumes to represent a particular character from a manga, anime, video game or movie. For the most part, the images in the category "Pop culture" were given positive marks. However, it was often the case that the same image was rated as positive by one respondent but perceived as neutral or negative by other students. Such mixed ratings were most often given to the images "manga", "anime" and "J-pop". Despite a low mean valence value, this category was among the three top salient groups of images of Japan (SR=0.395; SI=3). Next, the category "History" contained the images "World War II", "samurai" and "karayuki-san" (the term for women who in the late 19th and early 20th centuries travelled from impoverished regions of Japan to work as prostitutes in South East Asian countries). Among the total five images in this category, three images – "samurai" (0), "karayuki-san" (−1) and "World War II" (−1) – were given either neutral or negative ratings. These low marks decreased the mean valence value or overall favourability of the category. In addition to its low favourability, the category "History" was among the least salient groups of images of Japan (SI=0.111; SR=11).

Two categories of images of Japan had negative mean valence values. This is because all of the images they contained were marked as negative. Moreover, the lowest possible rating −2 prevailed among the marks. These categories were "Natural and man-made disasters" (MV=−1.67; MVR=14) and "Society problems" (MV=−1.70; MVR=15). The former group of images contained references to "earthquake", "tsunami", "radiation", "nuclear power plant" and "Fukushima Daiichi". It should be noted, however, that these negative images were placed almost at the bottom of the students' lists, which might indicate that they did not occupy a prominent position in the students' collective mind (SI=0.089; SR=13). In contrast, the images forming the category "Society problems" (e.g., the "ageing population", "death caused by overwork", "pornography", "suicide" and "yakuza") tended to come to the minds of the students more rapidly, which resulted in this category's middle position in salience (SI=0.144; SR=9).

Language learners' mental images of Korea

The 24 learners of Korean in this study provided 188 (N=188) mental images of Korea. The longest list of images contained 21 (n=21) items, while the three shortest lists consisted of 4 (n=4) answers each. On average, the students gave 11 answers per one list of images, and the mode value was 5.

Consensual stereotypes of Korea

There were 37 consensual stereotypes among the mental images of Korea (see Table A4.5 in Appendix 2). This finding indicates that the students had a diversified palette of mental imagery of the target language country.

The most widely shared consensual stereotype was "K-dramas" (a term referring to television mini-series produced in South Korea), as it was mentioned by 12 respondents. The following in popularity image was "K-pop" (a genre of South Korean popular music that enjoys world-wide fandom), which was mentioned by six students. It is worth noting that many of the consensual stereotypes of Korea were mentioned with a high frequency. For example, the answers "Jeju Island" (a popular tourist destination among Malaysians), "hangul" (the unique Korean alphabet) and "Park Geun-hye" (the controversial former president of South Korea, and the first woman to hold this post) were each given by four respondents. Other images that were shared by more than two students referred to various Korean traditional dishes, such as kimchi (fermented, salty and spicy vegetables served as a side dish), kimbap (cooked rice and other fillings rolled in dried seaweed) and ramyeon (a type of instant noodles). The expressions *saranghae* (meaning "I love you") and *annyeonghaseyo* (a greeting) were mentioned by three respondents, as was the case with the references to a traditional Korean dress, *hanbok*, King Sejong the Great (a historical figure), the Namsan Tower (a landmark in Seoul) and Samsung (a South Korean multinational conglomerate and brand). Interestingly, three students came up with the image "ppali-ppali culture" (*ppali-ppali* means "hurry up!", quickly!" or "faster!" in Korean), which reflects a peculiar characteristic of contemporary South Korean culture that places a high value on speed and efficiency.

Not all of the most frequently mentioned consensual stereotypes were highly salient. For example, even though the image "ppali-ppali culture" was mentioned by three students, its salience was rather low (SI=0.042; SR=26). The top salient consensual stereotypes of Korea predominantly referred to Korean pop culture and cuisine. Quite notably, the image "K-pop" had a very high salience index, 0.821, which means that almost all of the respondents had placed this image at or near the top of their individual lists of images. In fact, "K-pop" is the image with the highest salience index in this entire study. As to the favourability parameters, almost all of the consensual stereotypes of Korea had positive mean valence values. This means that the positive ratings +2 and +1 were the predominant marks given by the respondents. The highest in favourability consensual stereotypes were "*annyeonghaseyo*", "food", "safe" and "Olympic games". The lowest in favourability images were "Park Geun-hye" and "plastic surgery". It should be noted that occupying the 16th and 17th positions in salience, the two negative images were relatively prominent in the collective mind of the students who had shared these images. As to the stereotype accuracy, the findings allow to conclude that the language learners had highly accurate mental images of Korea: 30 out of 37 consensual stereotypes referred either to specific sites in

Korea or to people and various phenomena, mostly cultural, originating from this country.

Categories of images of Korea

The next step in the analysis was to classify the mental images of Korea into larger categories. Thirteen categories of images were formed, not including the category "Others" (see Table A4.6 in Appendix 2). The highest in favourability category was labelled "Affective reaction" (MV=1.67; MVR=1). It contained the images "attractive", "beautiful" and "great!" which were all rated either +2 or +1. The fact that the students provided a sufficient number of abstract affectively charged responses that explicitly expressed their positive reaction toward the words "Korea" and "Koreans", and even formed a distinct category of images, is worthy to mention. Though this category was among the least salient groups of images of Korea (SI=0.076; SR=12), it still merits a mention that some respondents had shared their positive feelings toward the target language country, even if these images came as an afterthought. A slightly lower in favourability category was named "History" (MV=1.60; MVR=2). It contained references to "history", "King Sejong" and "Sejong the Great". All images in this category were given positive ratings +2 or +1. Despite the high favourability parameters, this group of images was among the least salient categories (SI=0.121; SR=11). Closely following in favourability was the category "Food" (MV=1.56; MVR=3), which was the most voluminous (n=25) and most salient (SI=0.482; SR=2) category of images of Korea. Besides several non-specific answers, such as "Korean food", the category included references to popular-in-Malaysia Korean dishes, such as "kimchi", "kimbap", "bibimbap", "ramyeon", "samgetang" (chicken soup with ginseng), "samyang" (instant noodle brand), "tteokkbakki" (spicy rice cakes), "yukgaejang" (spicy beef soup), "japchae" (stir-fried glass noodles and vegetables) and "mandu" (Korean dumplings). None of these images was rated negatively; only one respondent gave a neutral rating 0 to the image "kimchi".

The category "Traditional culture" was found to have high favourability (MV=1.55; MVR=4) and salience (SI=0.351; SR=3). Among the images included in this category were "hanbok", "hanggul", "Arirang" (a folk song with almost 600 years of history and which is considered the unofficial national anthem of Korea) and "chuseok" (a traditional harvest festival and a major holiday in Korea). The following in favourability category was "K-pop, K-drama and entertainment" (MV=1.52; MVR=5). It was the most voluminous (n=42) and the top salient (SI=0.715; SR=1) category of images of Korea. Though some of the images included in this cluster were rather general (e.g., "K-dramas", "K-pop" and "actors") the majority of the responses were specific, which attests to the students' good knowledge of and familiarity with Korean pop culture. For example, there were several references to popular Korean TV dramas (e.g., *Winter Sonata*), to variety shows (e.g., *Running Man* and *2 Days & 1 Night*) and to an international mega hit song, "Gangnam Style". Other images in this category referred to South Korean bands, such as "BTS", "Exo", "Wanna One", "Big Bang", "VIXX" and "SNSD". There was one reference to "trot", which is a genre of Korean popular music, and two references to the largest South Korean entertainment company, "SM Entertainment". The overwhelming majority of images in the category "K-pop, K-drama and entertainment" were rated positively by the respondents; only three students gave the neutral rating 0 to their answers "K-drama", "K-pop" and "Big Bang". It should be noted that the respondents not only provided an impressive number of images pertaining to Korean pop culture: these images tended to readily come to the collective mind of the students, which resulted in very high salience parameters of this category. Its salience index, 0.715, was the highest index for a category of images in this entire study.

The categories "Language" and "Fashion and cosmetics" had the same, and rather high, favourability parameters (MV=1.50; MVR=6). They were also close in their salience ranks, although the images pertaining to Korean language were slightly more prominent in the collective mind of the students (SI=0.214; SR=7) compared to the images referring to fashion and cosmetics (SI=0.134; SR=8). The images in the latter category were, for the most part, rather general (e.g., "fashion", "cosmetics" and "make up"), and all of them were rated positively. The majority of the answers in the category "Language" consisted of Korean words written in the Latin script; they included the greeting "*annyeonghaseyo*", the expression of thanks "*kamsahamnida*" and the phrase "*saranghae*", which can be translated into English as "I love you". Some of the students wrote "hangul" (the name of the Korean letters in the alphabet), while others mentioned "hanja" (Chinese characters incorporated into the Korean language). One student had shared the image "honorific", which refers to the important cultural and linguistic requirement of addressing other people in a proper manner, while one more respondent simply stated "language". "Hanja" was the only image that received the neutral rating 0; all other images in this category were rated positively. The category "Language" occupied a middle position in salience (SI=0.214; SR=7).

The following in favourability category "Economy and technology" (MV=1.40; MVR=8) contained only five images and had rather low salience (SI=0.129; SR=9). This is an unexpected finding, especially in view that Korea is included among the world's leading nations in economic development and technological advancement. Among the images in this category were references to Korea being an "economically advanced" country and "the 11th world largest economy". One student mentioned "*chaebol*", which is a Korean word for large industrial conglomerates that are run either by a family or individual persons. This was the only image with the neutral rating 0; the rest of the images in this category were rated +2 and +1. The next, and slightly lower in favourability, category was "Cities, geographical names and sites" (MV=1.37; MVR=9). It contained a comparatively large number of images (n=19) and was among the top five most salient categories of images of Korea (SI=0.227; SR=5). To give more details, this category contained several references to the capital city of Korea, Seoul, to the famous port-city Busan and to the city of Incheon. Several students mentioned Jeju Island, a popular tourist destination among Malaysians, and Nami Island, which is famous for its half-moon shape. In addition, several references were made to the Han River, which is a major river in Korea and an ancient trade route to China. Some of the mental images recalled prominent urban landmarks, such as the Namsan Tower in Seoul. One student mentioned "Lotte World theme park", which is a large recreation complex in Seoul attracting millions of visitors every year. The majority of the images in the category "Cities, geographical names and sites" were rated positively. Only one student gave a negative rating (−1) to the image "Namsan Tower".

Some students included South Korean brands in their lists of images. These responses formed the category "Brands", which occupied a middle position in favourability (MV=1.33; MVR=10) and salience (SI=0.128; SR=10). Among the brands recalled by the students were "LG", "Samsung", "Hyundai" and "Korean Air". The majority of these images were rated positively, and the only neutral rating was given to the image "smartphone Samsung". The following in favourability category was "Modern society and lifestyle" (MV=1.16; MVR=0.264). It contained 25 images and was one of the most voluminous and salient (SI=0.264; SI=4) categories of images of Korea. Some of the images made references to the public transportation in Korea (e.g., "subway", "bus"), to the perceived safety, cleanliness and efficiency permeating life in the target language country (e.g., "safe", efficient", "fast", "ppali-ppali culture", "clean" and "high speed internet"). Some of the students simply mentioned "society", while others noted less positive realities of life in South Korea, including the "ageing population", "drinking culture", "education fever", "materialism" and "plastic surgery". Interestingly, only a few of the images that could be perceived as negative were marked as such by the students. For example, somewhat unexpectedly, the image "drinking culture" was marked +2, and the image "materialism" was rated 0. The negative rating −1 (which is not the lowest possible rating in this study) was given only to the images "education fever", "plastic surgery" and "stress".

The category "People", despite occupying a middle position in favourability (MV=1.11; MVR=12), was among the largest clusters of images of Korea. Among its 18 images, the former president of South Korea, Park Geun-hye, was mentioned twice. One student rated this image as negative (−2), while another gave it the neutral rating, 0. Another former president of South Korea, Park Chung-hee, was also mentioned twice. The students who mentioned this image gave one neutral and one positive rating (+1), respectively. Many of the responses in this category made references to South Korean pop singers (e.g., Kang Daniel, Lee Seung-gi and Ong Seong-wu); all of these images received the highest possible rating, +2. Interestingly, some students mentioned the names of the language instructors and lecturers who came from South Korea, and gave these images the highest rating, +2. Among the images in this cluster, only two pertained to the physical appearance of Korean people. These images were "pretty girls" and "handsome boys"; they were rated positively (+2). Only one image referred to the perceived character of the Korean people. This image was "hardworking", and it received the neutral rating 0. In salience, the category "People" occupied a middle position (SI=0.216; SR=6). This indicates that while the images referring to Korean people were numerous, they were not among the first images to come to the students' minds when they were answering the open-ended question.

The only category of images of Korea that did not have a positive mean valence value was "Divided country" (MV=0.00; MVR=13). It contained such responses as "(Korea is) divided in two countries", "(South Korea is) separated from North Korea" and "DMZ" (an acronym for Korean Demilitarized Zone). Almost all of these images were rated as neutral. Only one image, namely, "(South Korea is) separated from North Korea", received a negative rating (−1). It should be noted that this category was not only the least favourable but also the least salient (SI=0.059; SR=13) cluster of images. This means that the students who provided these images tended to recall them as an afterthought and, as a result, these images were placed at the end, or close to the end, of their lists.

Language learners' mental images of Myanmar

The 18 learners of the Myanmar language who participated in this study provided 126 ($N=126$) mental images of the target language country. The longest list contained 14 images while the shortest one had only 2 responses. On average, the students produced 7 images per list and the mode value was 5.

Consensual stereotypes of Myanmar

As in the rest of this study, the images of Myanmar mentioned by two or more language learners were considered consensual stereotypes of the target language country. In total, 19 consensual stereotypes of Myanmar were identified (see Table A4.7 in Appendix 2). The most frequently mentioned and the most salient (SI=0.292; SR=1) consensual stereotype was "rich culture" (n=8). It was followed in salience by the images "South East Asian country" (SI=0.211; SR=2), "Buddhist country" (SI=0.210; SR=3), "Ethnic problems" (SI=0.200; SR=4) and the "Rohingya people" (SI=0.192; SR=5). Notably, two among these top five most salient and frequently mentioned consensual stereotypes of Myanmar had negative mean valence values. The image "Ethnic problems" had the lowest possible favourability value (MV=−2), while the image "Rohingya people" had the mean valence value −1. Other consensual stereotypes that had negative mean valence values were "Lack of modern facilities" (SI=0.05; SR=15; MV=−2.00), "Military government" (SI=0.035; SR=16; MV=−2.00) and "Not a well-known country" (SI=0.02; SR=19: MV=−1.50). However, all of these images had a low frequency of mention (n=2) and low salience parameters. Besides, the fact that the students perceived a lack of information about Myanmar in a negative light does not attest to their negative perception of the target language country per se.

An additional insight into the students' mental imagery of Myanmar can be gained when comparisons are made between the favourability and salience parameters of the consensual stereotypes of Myanmar. Thus, more than half of the highly salient consensual stereotypes, or the images that tended to promptly come to the students' collective mind, occupied either middle or the lowest positions in favourability. At the same time, the two most favourable consensual stereotypes – "Traditional clothes" (SI=0.104; SR=10; MV=2.00; MVR=1) and "Festivals" (SI=0.032; SR=17; MV=2.00; MVR=1) – had a comparatively low salience. In other words, these highly favourable images tended to come to the minds of the respondents as an afterthought and be placed closer to the end of their lists. Concerning accuracy of the stereotypical images, only four of the nineteen consensual stereotypes of Myanmar could be placed at the "unique" end of the "common–unique" continuum. These images were "Rohingya people", "Burmese history", "thanaka" and "Aung San Suu Kyi". Overall, the students' mental imagery of Myanmarwas not highly accurate and specific.

Categories of images of Myanmar

In the next step of the analysis, all mental images of Myanmar were classified into seven categories, excluding the category "Others" (see Table A4.8 in Appendix 2). The category with the highest favourability parameters was

"Culture and history" (MV=1.65; MVR=1). Notably, it was also the most voluminous (*n*=23) and the second most salient (SI=0.418; SR=2) group of mental images of Myanmar. These findings indicate that the images pertaining to various aspects of Myanmar's culture and history were not only numerous, but they also tended to promptly come to the minds of the respondents. Among the images placed in this category were "rich culture", "traditional culture", "traditional attire" and "nice traditional clothes". Some students mentioned "traditional festivals" held in the country, and one respondent elaborated that the Burmese New Year is celebrated in April and that "the festivities are similar to the water festival in Thailand". Other culture-orientated images placed in this category were "food", "romantic films" and "thanaka powder" (a natural cosmetic produced from ground bark and wood). The images pertaining to Myanmar's history included "(Myanmar) has its own history", "historical places" and "history of Burmese people". Though somewhat general and lacking in substance, the mental images referring to Myanmar's rich cultural heritage and history were rated as positive (+2 and +1) by the students, except for the image "thanaka powder", which was rated as neutral by one respondent.

The category "Religion and religious sites" occupied the second position in favourability (MV=1.46; MVR=2). It contained such images as "Buddhism", "the Buddha", "Buddhist country", "monks", "religion", "religious places", "pagodas" and "Shwezigon Pagoda". Almost all of the images in this category were rated positively by the language learners; the only negatively rated image referred to a perceived lack of religious freedom in Myanmar. This category occupied a middle position in salience (SR=0.233; SI=5). The following in favourability category, "Language" (MV=1.36; MVR=3), had a rather high salience (SI=0.3; SR=4). This indicates that the images related to the Myanmar language tended to come to the minds of the respondents more readily compared to the references to religion. This is not surprising, as all of the respondents were learning the Myanmar language at the time of data collection. The majority of the images in this category were the descriptions of the perceived qualities of the Myanmar language, such as "interesting language" and "difficult language". Several students wrote words and expressions in the Myanmar language and provided their Latin transliteration (e.g., "*ngarr*", meaning "five"). Some of the students opined that the Myanmar language "originates from Sanskrit" and has a "Sanskrit writing system"; these were the only images that were rated as neutral. The overwhelming majority of the responses in this cluster were rated +2, and there were no images with the negative ratings.

The following in favourability category was "Country location, country size and standing" (MV=0.60; MVR=4). Quite notably, there was a sharp drop in the mean valence value of this cluster (MV=0.60) compared to the immediately preceding in favourability group of images, "Language" (MV=1.36). This large decline was due to the many negatively and several neutrally rated images that formed this category. Among such images were "not a very safe country" (rated −1), "not a choice to travel" (−1) and "not a well-known country" (rated −2 and −1 by the two respondents who provided this answer). The images "the country near China and India" and "South East Asian country" were rated as neutral by almost all students. Among the category's positively rated images were "big country", "strategic place", "the largest country in mainland South East Asia", "South East Asia", "close to India, Bangladesh, China and Thailand", "ASEAN" and "interesting country to travel". The overwhelming majority of the latter images were given the highest possible rating, +2. It should be noted that the category "Country location, country size and standing" was among the top three most sizeable ($n=20$) and most salient (SR=0.409; SI=3) groups of mental images of Myanmar.

The category "People and population" (MV=0.38; MVR=5), which occupied the fifth position in favourability, contained several references to Aung San Suu Kyi, the world renowned politician and Nobel Peace Prize laureate. This image was rated +2 by almost all of the respondents, and only one student gave it the neutral mark. Some of the mental images in this category pertained to the perceived character of the Myanmar people (e.g., "people are really kind"), their religious affiliations ("Burmese people are Buddhists"), their perceived behaviours and actions, such as "women apply white powder to their faces", "the way people dress", "people chew betel and spit it out" and "they don't understand English". The latter two images were rated −2. Also, two respondents provided the image "large population", which they rated 0 and +1, respectively. As the salience parameters indicate, the category "People and population" was among the least prominent groups of images of Myanmar (SI=0.181; SR=6).

Two categories of mental images of Myanmar – "Multi-ethnic country, ethnic issues, political situation" (MV=−0.81; MVR=6) and "Economy, lack of technology" (MV=−1.13; MVR=7) – had negative mean valence values. Notably, the category "Multi-ethnic country, ethnic issues, political situation" occupied the top position in salience (SR=0.479; SI=1) and the second place in number of images ($n=21$). Among very few positively rated images in this category were the references to a multi-ethnic composition of Myanmar (e.g., "a lot of ethnic groups", "different ethnic groups" and "unique tribes"). The neutral rating 0 was given to the images "their ethnic Rohingya come to Malaysia", "the Rohingya refugees in Malaysia" and the "Saffron Revolution", which referred to political protests in Myanmar in the year 2007. The majority of images in this category, including the images "ethnic cleansing", "military government", "the Rohingya issue", "the civil

Language learners' country stereotypes 73

war" and "the army", were rated as "strongly negative" (−2) by the students. In other words, a substantial number of the images of Myanmar that came to the students' collective mind most readily and frequently were negative. Finally, the category labelled "Economy, lack of technology" (MV=− 1.13; MVR=7) with its eight images was the smallest group of images of the target language country. As can be deduced from the negative mean valence, the majority of the images were given negative ratings. These images included "poor country", "economic problems", "poor living standards" and "lack of modern technologies". One response – "Burma has now open door policy" – received a positive rating (+1), and the laconic answer "economy" was given the neutral rating 0.

Language learners' mental images of Thailand

In total, the 22 students learning Thai provided 177 images of the target language country. The longest list of images contained 23 responses and the shortest one had 3 images. The average number of images per individual list was 9 and the mode value was 6.

Consensual stereotypes of Thailand

The number of consensual stereotypes, or the images shared by two or more respondents, was 36 (n=36) (see Table A4.9 in Appendix 2). This finding attests to a rich kaleidoscope of the language learners' mental imagery of the target language country. The most frequently mentioned consensual stereotypes were "food", "Thai movies" and "beautiful people". Each of these images was mentioned by seven respondents. Another popular image was "tom yam" (a spicy and sour soup), which appeared in six individual lists (n=6). It was closely followed in frequency (n=5) by the images "Krabi" (a province in southern Thailand), "*Muay Thai*" (Thai boxing), "horror movies", "friendly people" and a somewhat general reference to "places to visit".

The three most salient consensual stereotypes of Thailand were "tom yam" (SI=0.379; SR=1), "food" (SI=0.355; SR=2) and "Thai movies" (SI=0.213; SR=3). Notably, "food" and "Thai movies", besides being highly salient, were also among the most favourable consensual stereotypes as they had the highest possible mean valence value (MV=2.00). This means that all students who mentioned these images gave them the top rating, +2. Other consensual stereotypes with the highest favourability value – but lower in salience – were the greeting word "*sawasdee*", "festivals", "Thai people", "loyalty to their king", "actors" and "beaches". Although the overwhelming number of consensual stereotypes (or 34 out of total 36) were positive, two had negative mean valence values. They were "*pondan*" (a Malay word that could be translated into English as "transvestite") (MV=-1.33) and "war" (MV=-2.00). It should be noted that these two consensual stereotypes were also among the least salient images of Thailand. Thus, the image "*pondan*" was ranked as 32nd in salience (SI=0.036; SR=32) and "war" was the 35th in salience rank (SI=0.024; SR=35). This means that these images tended to come to the students' collective mind as an afterthought and, as a result, they were written in the end – or very close to the end – of the individual lists of images. Regarding the accuracy of stereotypes, 13 out of 36 consensual images of Thailand pertained to phenomena to be found in or originating from Thailand (e.g., "tom yam" soup, "Muay Thai", "Krabi", "Hat Yai", "Bangkok", "Thai language"). These images could be placed at the extreme "unique" end of the "common–unique" continuum. Several other images, such as "market on boats", "loyalty to their king" and "water festival", could be located very near this end point. Based on these findings, the students' collective mental imagery of Thailand could be considered as rather accurate.

Categories of images of Thailand

In the following step of the analysis, all mental images of Thailand were divided into nine larger categories, excluding the category "Others" (see Table A4.10 in Appendix 2). Three categories with the highest favourability parameters were "Food" (MV=1.80; MVR=1), "Beautiful islands, beaches, sea" (MV=1.62; MVR=2) and "Popular culture" (MV=1.59; MVR=3). It is interesting to note that "Food" was also the second most salient category of images of Thailand (SI=0.497; SR=2) after the category "Traditional culture, cultural symbols, religion" (SI=0.513; SR=1). This means that the students tended to rapidly recall the images pertaining to Thai food and placed these images at the top, or very close to the top, of their lists. It also should be noted that besides the general references to "Thai food", "street food", "delicious food" or simply "food", the students provided the names of particular – and very popular in Malaysia – dishes. These included "tom yam", "som tam", "papaya salad" and "Thai fried rice". All images in the category "Food" were given the positive ratings +2 or +1. Next, the category "Beautiful islands, beaches, sea" (MV=1.62; MVR=2) contained the references to "beautiful islands", "beautiful beaches", "the beauty of the islands in Krabi" and "beautiful beaches in Krabi". All these images were given the positive marks +2 and +1. The following in favourability category "Popular culture" (MV=1.59; MVR=3) was dominated by the references to "horror movies", which were rated either +2 or given the neutral rating 0. Other images included "movies", "interesting dramas" and "Thai song". Except for the neutral rating 0 given to the images "horror movies" and "horror movies that seem real", all responses in this category were rated positively (+2 or +1). The category "Language" also had comparatively high favourability parameters (MV=1.56; MVR=4). Many of the images included in this group were worded in a way to reflect the students' positive feelings about the target language (e.g., "a very interesting language to learn", "attractive language" and "the language that is nice to hear"). Several responses were rather general in nature, such as "their language" and "Thai script", while some students wrote as a response the Thai greeting "*sawasdee*". All images in this category were rated either +2 or +1. Next, the category "People" (MV=1.53; MVR=5), which closely followed in favourability, was the largest group of images of Thailand (*n*=30). The majority of the images referred to the appearance of Thai people and described them as "beautiful people", "handsome people" and people who have "beautiful skin". Some of the images pertained to "handsome celebrities", "handsome guys in Thai dramas" and "beautiful girls in Thai movies". There were also images that referred to the perceived character, attitudes and behaviour of Thai people. Among these images were "friendly people", "polite people", "people have a nice smile", "soft spoken people", "people are loyal to their king" and "(they) cannot speak English". Some respondents simply stated "Siamese people". The only negatively rated image in this category was "(they) cannot speak English", which was given the mark −1. Despite being the largest group of images of Thailand, the category "People" occupied the third place in salience (SI=0.373; SR=3).

The references to Thai cities, tourist sites and travel destinations formed the category "Cities, sites, places to visit" (MV=1.44; MVR=6). This was the most salient category of images of Thailand (SI=0.513; SR=1). However, it ranked as only seventh in favourability. This could be due to the negative rating −1 assigned by some students to the images "water festival", "Bangkok" and "Muay Thai". Also, almost half of the images in this group were given the ratings +1 and 0, and not the top rating +2. As to the category's contents, there were references to Bangkok (the capital of Thailand), Hat Yai (a Thai city near the Malaysian border and a popular shopping destination among Malaysians) and the historical city of Chiang Mai in northern Thailand. Several students mentioned unspecified "amazing tourist spots", "nice places to visit", "places to visit" and "places". Next in the favourability parameters was the category "Traditional culture, cultural symbols, religion" (MV=1.20; MVR=7). The most frequently mentioned image in this group was "Muay Thai", which is a traditional Thai combat sport (also known as Thai boxing) that enjoys worldwide popularity. Several students provided the images "their culture", "a very different culture compared to Malaysian", "traditional clothes", "the water festival" and "Songkran" (a festival marking the arrival of the Thai New Year and the coming of spring). There were also several images pertaining to religion, namely, "temples", "Buddhism" and "monks".

The category "Contemporary lifestyle and society" (MV=0.95; MVR=8) was among the lowest in favourability groups of images of Thailand. Interestingly, it was also the third in size (n=21). This category contained a mélange of responses, including "shopping", "spa and massage", "their university uniform", "good and effective education system", "Thai bureaucracy", "plastic surgery", "*tuk-tuk*" (a popular type of urban transportation) and "Thai food festivals". For the most part, the images in this category were rated positively; the neutral rating 0 was given to the answers "shopping complex" and "plastic surgery". Among the negatively rated images was "*pondan*" (which can be translated from Malay as "transvestite"); it was given the marks −2 and −1 by the respondents. Despite a relatively large number of images, the category "Contemporary lifestyle and society" was among the two lowest in salience (SI=0.15; SR=8) groups of images of Thailand. The low salience parameters indicate that the students tended to recall the images placed in this category as an afterthought and, as a result, wrote these images at the end of their lists.

The category "Country descriptions" had the lowest, albeit positive, mean valence value (MV=0.91; MVR=9). It was also the smallest group of images of Thailand (n=11). Among the images placed in this category were "a very beautiful country", "the only country in South East Asia that was never colonized", "a worldwide country" and "[a] powerful country that has a strong economy among South East Asian countries". Some students mentioned that Thailand has "interesting history" and "interesting politics". Almost all images in this category were rated positively (+2 and +1). The only negatively rated image was "the country that always has war" (−2), which does not do justice to Thailand's history. The response "united front of democracy against dictatorship" received the neutral rating 0.

Language learners' mental images of Vietnam

The 13 learners of Vietnamese in this study provided 76 (N=76) images of the target language country. The longest individual list contained 11 (n=11) responses, and the shortest one had only 3 images (n=3). On average, each student produced 6 images and the mode value was 5.

Consensual stereotypes of Vietnam

Eight consensual stereotypes, or the images mentioned by two and more respondents, were distinguished among the 76 mental images of Vietnam (see Table A4.11 in Appendix 2). These consensual stereotypes were "Ho Chi Minh city",

"Hanoi", "Vietnam War", "Vietnamese food", "communism", "traditional outfit", "easy language" and "water puppets". The most salient consensual stereotype was "Ho Chi Minh City" (SI=0.424; SR=1); it was followed by the image "Hanoi" (SI=0.282; SR=2). It should be noted that two of the eight consensual stereotypes of Vietnam had negative mean valence values. These images were "communism" (MV=−0.67) and "Vietnam war" (MV=−0.50) and, notably, they were among the five most salient consensual stereotypes of the target language country. At the same time, the most favourable consensual stereotypes of Vietnam – "traditional outfit" (MV=1.50) and "water puppets" (MV=1.50) – were among the least salient. This finding indicates that the negatively perceived references to communism and the Vietnam War tended to appear in the collective mind of the respondents readily, while the positive culturally related images arrived as an afterthought. Regarding stereotype accuracy, four out of eight consensual stereotypes, namely, "Ho Chi Minh city", "Hanoi", "Vietnam war" and "Vietnamese food", could be described as unique images; the image "water puppets" could also be placed near the "unique" end of the "common–unique" continuum. These findings indicate that although very limited in scope, the images of Vietnam were rather accurate.

Categories of images of Vietnam

Next, all mental images of Vietnam provided by the language learners were classified into larger categories. Ten categories were formed, with the exception of the category "Others" (see Table A4.12 in Appendix 2). The category with the highest mean valence value was "Weather and seasons" (MV=2.00; MVR=1). This means that all images that formed this group, namely, "cold weather", "Vietnam has four seasons" and "winter", were assigned the highest possible rating, +2, by the students. Interestingly, it was also the least salient category of images of Vietnam (SI=0.056; SR=10). In other words, these images tended to come to the students' minds as an afterthought and were placed in the end of their lists. Next in favourability was the category "Language" (MV=1.65; MVR=2). It was also the most voluminous (n=17) and the second most salient group of images (SI=0.309; SR=2). Among the images forming this category were the language learners' opinions and beliefs about the target language (e.g., "the language is easy to learn", "Vietnamese is similar to the Chinese language" and "the language is totally different from the Malay language"). Some students responded that knowledge of Vietnamese was "good for future employment" and the language was "interesting to learn". All images in this category were given the positive marks +1 and +2. A higher salience of this category attests to the fact that the students tended to recall the images pertaining to the target language quite readily and placed them at the top or near the top of their lists.

The category "Culture and ways of life" was the third most favourable (MV=1.08; MVR=3) and the second largest (n=12) category of images of Vietnam. It was also among the three top salient groups (SI=0.274; SR=3). Some of the images in this category were quite general (e.g., "culture" and "Vietnamese culture"). Among specific references to the target culture were "water puppets", "traditional hats that the Vietnamese wear" and "the traditional clothes". All of these images were rated positively by the respondents. As to the mental representations pertaining to the perceived ways of life in Vietnam, one student mentioned that "men respect women" while other respondents came up with the images "heavy traffic in the city" and "some places [are] a bit dirty". The latter two images were rated −1. Next in favourability were the categories "Cities" (MV=1.00; MVR=4; SI=0.421; SR=1), "People" (MV=1.00; MVR=4; SI=0.161; SR=8) and "Economy" (MV=1.00; MVR=4; SI=0.086; SR=9). Although these three categories had the same favourability parameters, by salience measures the group "Cities" (SI=0.421; SR=1) occupied the top position and the other two categories were among the least salient groups of images. This means that the majority of the students in this study tended to readily recall the images referring to Ho Chi Minh City, Hanoi and Saigon (the former name of Ho Chi Ming City) and placed these images at the top of their lists. The favourability rating given to these images were either positive or neutral. For example, some students rated the images "Hanoi" and "Ho Chi Minh city" as positive (+2 or +1) while several respondents assigned to the same images the neutral rating 0.

Images forming the category "People" referred to the perceived character and behaviour of Vietnamese people (e.g., "people are active" and "people are kind"), including their resilience in the face of challenges (e.g., "people fought against the colonial powers", "they won the Vietnam War against the USA"). All of these images were marked as positive. Some images in the category "People" received the negative mark −1; among them were "inflexible people" and "Vietnamese people like to eat exotic food". Next, the category "Economy" consisted of the images "economic development of Vietnam", "marketable country" and "Vietnam opened its market through the *Doi Moi* policy". These images were rated as either positive or neutral. The next in favourability parameters category, "Food" (MV=0.75; MVR=7), included only general responses, such as "food" and "Vietnamese food". To match somewhat vague notions about Vietnamese cuisine, the salience of this category was rather low (SI=0.182; SR=6). The marks given to the food related images were mixed and ranged from +2 to −1.

The category with the lowest positive favourability value was "History" (MV=0.20; MVR=8). It contained references to "Vietnamese history", "the history of Vietnam War" and "Vietnamese War". It should be noted that the lowest mean valence value of the category does not necessarily mean that the language learners had less positive attitudes toward this country-related aspect. Rather, the category's comparatively low favourability was due to the fact that the images pertaining to "Vietnamese War" were given, as may be expected, the lowest rating, −2. The images of a more general nature (e.g., "Vietnamese history") were marked positively. Despite the lower favourability, the category "History" was among the more salient clusters of images of Vietnam (SI=0.236; SR=4).

There were two categories of images that had negative mean valence value, namely, "Political system" (MV=−0.50; MVR=9; SI=0.192; SR=5) and "China's influence" (MV=−0.50; MVR=9; SI=0.173; SR=7). The former category included the images "communism", "communist country" and "Vietnam is a socialist country". Most of these images were rated as neutral; only the image "communist country" received the lowest possible negative rating, −2. Among the images forming the category "China's influence" were "a country related to ancient China" and "[Vietnam] has a similar culture with China"; these responses were given the neutral mark 0. Also included in this group were the images "[Vietnam] was conquered by China" and "huge influence of China in [Vietnam's] history", which were both rated −1. The two categories occupied a middle position in prominence, as reflected in their salience parameters.

A discussion of the findings on the language learners' mental images of the target language countries

Findings from the analysis of the stereotype content

The mental images of China, Japan, Korea, Myanmar, Thailand and Vietnam collected from the learners of the six target languages allowed for some interesting and worthwhile insights into the mental imagery or "pictures in the head" that the students have about the target language countries and the attitudes embedded in these images. Also, the findings afforded some valuable glimpses into the meaning(s) with which the learners filled the name of the target language country. The contents analysis revealed that the learners of Japanese, Korean and Thai languages had produced the greatest number of consensual stereotypes, which attests to their vivid and nuanced palettes of the mental imagery of the target language country. In other words, Individually and collectively, the learners of these languages attached richer meanings to the target country's name. The learners of the three languages not only generated the largest numbers of images, but they also produced, on average, between 12 and 9 images per individual student (see Table 4.1).

Table 4.1 Summary of the findings on the language learners' mental images of the target language countries

Target language country	Number of students	Total number of images	Average number of images per student	Number of consensual stereotypes	Composite mean valence (CompMV)
China	31	161	6	30	0.86
Japan	22	185	12	38	1.24
Korea	24	188	11	37	1.45
Myanmar	18	126	7	19	0.68
Thailand	22	177	9	36	1.45
Vietnam	13	76	6	8	1.04

The number of the consensual stereotypes of each of these countries, or the images shared by two and more students, were also impressive: 38 for Japan, 37 for Korea and 36 for Thailand.

The learners of Korean and Japanese languages held the most accurate "mental pictures" of the target language countries. The overwhelming majority of their consensual stereotypes referred to unique phenomena to be found in or originating from the target countries. However, in order to gain deeper insights into the students' mental imagery, it would be useful to not only consider how plentiful the images were but also to scrutinize what was present and what was lacking from the mosaic in the students' mental imagery. Such insights would be particularly useful for making empirically driven pedagogical decisions about developing the cultural component of a language program. Therefore, the categories of the images of each target language country would need to be further classified into broader country-related aspects. In this book, these aspects included a target language country's traditional culture, popular culture, arts, political realities, language, history, geography, economy, technology, people, food, affective reaction and modern realities. This selection is based on the existing taxonomies (Brijs, Bloemer and Kasper, 2011; Echtner and Ritchie, 1993). The findings presented in Table 4.2 indicate that the learners of Mandarin, Korean and Japanese languages had the most diversified and complete mental imagery of the target language countries as only one country-related aspect was found to be lacking from the students' images.

In the case of China, the missing country-related aspect was popular culture. Among the images of Korea, the references to the arts were lacking. As to Japan, the images pertaining to the arts and political realities did not contribute to the building blocks of the students' imagery of the target language country. Based on these findings, it could be proposed that the meanings of the words "Japan", "Korea" and "China" were comparatively rich,

Table 4.2 Categories of country images and absent country-related aspects

Country	Categories of images	Absent country-related aspects
China	Mysterious and complex country; Cuisine and food; Literature and poetry; Technology; Traditional culture and culture symbols; Social media and e-commerce; History; Advanced and developed country; Cities, places and sites; Modern, fast paced and strong country; Big country; Language; People; Large population; Political system and international position	popular culture
Japan	Modern lifestyle; Seasons; Economy; People; Technology and car makers; Social values; Traditional culture and culture symbols; Cities, places and sites; Food and beverages; Brands; Language; Pop culture; History; Natural and man-made disasters; Society issues	arts; political realities
Korea	Affective reaction; History; Food; Traditional culture; K-pop, K-drama and entertainment; Language; Fashion and cosmetics; Economy and technology; Cities, geographical names and sites; Brands; Modern society and lifestyle; People; Divided country	arts
Myanmar	Culture and history; Religion and religious sites; Language; Country location, country size and standing; People and population; Multi-ethnic country, ethnic issues, political situation; Economy, lack of technology	arts; popular culture; food
Thailand	Food; Beautiful islands, beaches, sea; Popular culture; Language; People; Cities, sites, places to visit; Traditional culture, cultural symbols, religion; Contemporary lifestyle and society; Country descriptions	arts; political realities; history; economy; technology
Vietnam	Weather and seasons; Language; Culture and ways of life; Cities; People; Economy; Food; History; Political system; China's influence	arts; popular culture; technology; modern realities

diversified and multifaceted for the students who learned Japanese, Korean and Mandarin languages. In comparison, there was a greater number of the missing country-related aspects in the mental imagery of the target language countries provided by the learners of Myanmar, Thai and Vietnamese languages. For example, the images pertaining to the arts, popular culture and food were not a part of the students' mental pictures of Myanmar. The facets missing from the language learners' mental imagery of Thailand included the arts, political realities, history, economy and technology. The missing pieces in the Vietnamese language learners' mental mosaic of the target language country were the arts, popular culture, technology and modern realities.

Regrettably, there is a lack of scholarly research on mental images that learners of Asian languages hold about target language countries. Therefore, the discussion here will be limited to comparing the current study's findings with outcomes of my own previous research. Quite similarly, the learners of Mandarin in the current and earlier study (Nikitina and Furuoka, 2013) provided a considerable share of images that pertained to Chinese traditional culture, China's history, its climate, landscape, economy, religion, contemporary politics, the Mandarin language and Chinese people. However, notably absent from the earlier study were the images of China being a technologically advanced, modern and fast-paced country that has a thriving social media and robust worldwide e-commerce. Such perceptions were prominent in the present study. Another difference in the findings was that the images provided by the participants in the current study indicated the students' awareness that China is a complex country. In my earlier study, the predominant images of China pertained to famous tourist sites (e.g., the "Great Wall of China"), to Chinese international pop culture and cultural icons.

As to the images of Japan and Korea, there was a greater concordance in the students' mental imagery across the current and earlier research (e.g., Nikitina and Furuoka, 2019; Nikitina and Paidi, 2019). This could be due to a smaller time lag between the studies. To be more specific, the learners of Japanese in both studies tended to provide either very few or no images at all that referred to the arts and political life in Japan. At the same time, compared to the earlier scholarly inquiry, the participants in the current study made more references to Japanese history, and they also mentioned a number of issues faced by modern Japanese society. As to the Korean language learners, their mental imagery of the target language country in the current and previous study was overwhelmingly dominated by the images referring to Korean pop culture (e.g., "K-pop", "Korean drama") and cuisine (e.g., "kimchi", "bibimbap"). Also, a considerable number of the references was made to popular tourist sites and cities in Korea, to the country's contemporary society, its modern lifestyle as well as to the Korean traditional culture and Korean language. Less frequently recalled were the images pertaining to Korean history, the economy and the country's technological advancements. Other notable omissions were the references to the arts and education.

Finding on the attitudes embedded in the mental images of the target language countries

As explained in Chapter 3, the overall attitudes embedded in the language learners' stereotypes of each of the six Asian countries were assessed by calculating the composite mean valence (CompMV) values. In other words, the sum total of all ratings given to the images of a target language country was divided by the number of images of this particular country. It was found that the composite mean valence values were positive for all countries, though there were notable differences in the strength of the students' positive attitudes (see Table 4.1). Thailand and Korea were the most positively perceived target language countries (CompMV=1.45); they were followed by Japan (CompMV=1.24) and Vietnam (CompMV=1.04). China's (CompMV=0.86) and Myanmar's (CompMV=0.68) composite mean valence values, while positive, were comparatively low and below 1.

A tentative proposition that could be put forward based on these findings is that there would exist positive associations between the students' mental images of the target language countries and their L2 motivation. It could also be proposed that these associations might be stronger and statistically significant for the data collected from the learners of Japanese, Korean and Thai languages compared to the data on China, Vietnam and Myanmar. The tentative proposition concerning the associations between the country stereotypes and L2 motivation is in line with the findings reported from the available empirical studies that examined language learners' attitudes toward target countries and cultures, and the relationship between these attitudes and L2 motivation (Csizér and Kormos, 2009; Gardner and Lambert, 1959, 1972; Nikitina, 2015, 2019; Yang, 2003). It should be noted, however, that with the exception of my own research (Nikitina, 2015, 2019), none of the earlier empirical investigations on language attitudes has included as a research variable the endogenous mental images or stereotypes that language learners have of target language countries. This lack of scholarly literature precludes making comparisons between the results obtained in this study and earlier empirical findings. The following section reports the findings concerning the tentative assumption of the positive and statistically significant associations between the language learners' attitudes toward the target language countries and their L2 motivation.

Findings from the statistical analysis: relationships between the country stereotypes and L2 motivation

Dimensions of the students' L2 motivation: results from the exploratory factor analysis (EFA)

First of all, the underlying structure of the students' L2 motivation was examined. The exploratory factor analysis (EFA) was performed for this purpose. Prior to running the EFA, the suitability of this statistical procedure was established. An examination of the correlation matrices revealed that all values were above the required level of .700. The results of the Kaiser–Meyer–Olkin (KMO) test of sampling adequacy and the Bartlett's chi-square test confirmed the suitability of the dataset for the EFA. The KMO coefficient at .815 was above the meritorious level .800, and the Bartlett's test of sphericity was significant ($\chi2$=564.235; p<.01). Thus, all the assumptions for the EFA test were fulfilled.

The outcome of the EFA revealed that there were four dimensions in the students' L2 motivation (see Table A4.13 in Appendix 2) and not three as had been originally proposed in Chapter 3. This result endorsed the finding concerning the structure of Malaysian language learners' L2 motivation reported in my earlier study (Nikitina, 2019). To be more specific, the items forming the original variable "General motivation" were separated into two distinct dimensions – "Effort" and "Perseverance". This result is consistent with the conceptualization of the general motivation that subsumed effort and perseverance. Though some of the newly formed four factors loaded items from different, as originally proposed, aspects of L2 motivation, the factors were sufficiently consistent and coherent; the constructs' reliability assessed by the Cronbach's alpha was good. Therefore, the four factors in this study were named as: (1) Instrumental orientation (Cronbach's α=.786), (2) Integrative orientation (Cronbach's α=.641), (3) Perseverance (Cronbach's α=.667) and (4) Effort (Cronbach's α=.550).[1] The ensuing statistical analyses, namely, the correlation test and the regression tests, were conducted on these four L2 motivation variables.

Findings from the correlation analysis

The relationship between the mental images of target language countries held by the students, the students' language attitudes and their L2 motivation was firstly assessed by the correlation analysis. The L2 motivation was measured by the variables Instrumental orientation, Integrative orientation, Perseverance and Effort. Due to the non-normality of the data and the presence of outliers, a Spearman's rank correlation test was performed. First of all, the aggregate data for all six countries were analyzed. The results of the Spearman's rank correlation test indicated that there existed positive and statistically significant relationships between the students' country stereotypes and each of the four dimensions of L2 motivation (see Table A4.14 in Appendix 2). The strongest association was found to exist between the stereotypes of the target language country and instrumental orientation (r_s=.342, p<.01), followed by the associations between the stereotypes and perseverance (r_s=.337, p<.01), integrative orientation (r_s=.217, p<.05) and effort (r_s=.189, p<.05). These findings support the tentative proposition put forward earlier in this chapter that assumed positive and statistically significant relationships between the country stereotypes and L2 motivation.

Next, a separate Spearman's rank correlation test was performed for the data on each of the six target language countries (see Table A4.15 in Appendix 2 for a summary of the findings). The tests yielded rather unexpected results. For example, except for the data on Thailand and Vietnam, no statistically significant relationship was found to exist between the language learners' country stereotypes and any of the four dimensions of L2 motivation. In the case of Vietnam, the country stereotypes had statistically significant positive relationships with the instrumental orientation (r_s=.622, p<.05), integrative orientation (r_s=.605, p<.05) and perseverance (r_s=.575, p<.05). The large effect size of each of these relationships, as reflected in the correlation coefficients above .50 (r_s>.50), attests to a considerable strength of these associations. As for the data on Thailand, the country stereotypes held by the students had a statistically significant positive and strong association with the perseverance dimension of L2 motivation (r_s=.464, p<.05). Another notable finding was that, despite a high overall favourability of the images of Korea (CompMV=1.45), not only positive statistical relationships between the country stereotypes and L2 motivation were lacking, but also the relationship between the country images and the effort dimension of L2 motivation was found to be negative (r_s=−.063). Another negative association between the study variables was detected in the data on Myanmar concerning the relationship between the country stereotypes and the perseverance dimensions (r_s=−.090).

In sum, while statistically significant positive relationships were found to exist between all variables in the aggregated data for the six target language countries, the picture from the analysis of the data on each individual target language country was more nuanced. Therefore, it would be enlightening to move beyond merely analyzing the associations between the variables and to see whether, on the whole, the country stereotypes had affected the language learners' L2 motivation. A regression analysis was performed for this purpose, and the findings are reported in the following section.

Findings from the regression analysis

The findings from the robust multiple regression analysis indicated that the mental images that the language learners held of the target language countries had a statistical effect on all four components of their L2 motivation (see Table A4.16 in Appendix 2). The narrow confidence intervals (CIs) indicate a good precision of the measurement. To be more specific, the effect of the country stereotypes was the greatest on the instrumental orientation ($\beta=.362$; $R^2=.131$; t-statistic=4.398, 95% CI [0.261; 0.355]). It was also found that the effect of the country stereotypes on the integrative orientation ($\beta=.289$; $R^2=.083$; t-statistic=3.415; 95% CI [0.249; 0.368]) was weaker compared to their impact on the perseverance dimension ($\beta=.352$; $R^2=.124$; t-statistic=4.253; 95% CI [0.351; 0.485]) but stronger than their effect on the effort aspect ($\beta=.255$; $R^2=.065$; t-statistic=2.987, 95% CI [0.185; 0.268]).

Overall, the findings from the statistical tests have lent support to the proposition that mental images the language learners hold about target language countries, their cultures and people would have associations with – and influence on – the students' L2 motivation. These findings are in line with the results reported in my earlier study that explored country images held by learners of European languages and the impact of these images on the students' L2 motivation (Nikitina, 2019). In the current study, the correlation analysis of the aggregated data on the six Asian target language countries detected positive and statistically significant associations between the students' country images and their L2 motivation. However, in the case of each particular country, the nature of this relationship was more nuanced. Furthermore, the results of the robust multiple regression analysis indicated that the mental images held by the students had a statistically significant influence on all four dimensions of their L2 motivation. However, the effect of the country stereotypes was the largest on the instrumental – and not on the integrative, as one could expect – orientation.

Note

1 As discussed in Chapter 3, acceptable values of Cronbach's α depend on the nature of a study and the academic field, and lower values of .60 and .50 might be acceptable in studies of a theoretical nature (Nunnally, 1967). However, the desired values would be expected to exceed .70 (Aron and Aron, 1999, p. 527).

References

Aron, A., & Aron, E. (1999). *Statistics for psychology* (2nd ed.). Upper Saddle River, NJ: Prentice Hall.

Brijs, K., Bloemer, J., & Kasper, H. (2011). Country-image discourse model: Unraveling meaning, structure, and function of country images. *Journal of Business Research, 64*(12), 1259–1269. doi: 10.1016/j.jbusres.2011.01.017

Csizér, K., & Kormos, J. (2009). Modelling the role of inter-cultural contact in the motivation of learning English as a foreign language. *Applied Linguistics, 30*(2), 166–185. doi: 10.1093/applin/amn025

Echtner, C. M., & Ritchie, J. R. B. (1993). The measurement of destination image: An empirical assessment. *Journal of Travel Research, 31*(4), 3–13.

Gardner, R. C., & Lambert, W. E. (1959). Motivational variables in second-language acquisition. *Canadian Journal of Psychology/Revue Canadienne de Psychologie, 13*(4), 266–272. doi: 10.1037/h0083787

Gardner, R. C., & Lambert, W. E. (1972). *Attitudes and motivation in second-language learning.* Rowley, MA: Newbury House Publishers.

Nikitina, L. (2015). Country stereotypes and L2 motivation: A study of French, German and Spanish language learners. *Studies in Linguistics, 37,* 483–509. https://doi.org/10.17002/sil.37.2015010.483

Nikitina, L. (2019). Do country stereotypes influence language learning motivation? A study among foreign language learners in Malaysia. *Moderna Språk, 113*(1), 58–79.

Nikitina, L., & Furuoka, F. (2013). "Dragon, kung fu and Jackie Chan . . .": Stereotypes about China held by Malaysian students. *Trames: Journal of the Humanities and Social Sciences, 17*(2), 175–195. doi: 10.3176/tr.2013.2.05

Nikitina, L., & Furuoka, F. (2019). Language learners' mental images of Korea: Insights for the teaching of culture in the language classroom. *Journal of Multilingual and Multicultural Development, 40*(9), 774–786. https://doi.org/10.1080/01434632.2018.1561704

Nikitina, L., & Paidi, R. (2019). *Images of Japan though time and space, and now and here.* Public lecture conducted on 27 March 2019, organized by Malaysian Association of Japanese Studies (MAJAS) and Japan Foundation, Kuala Lumpur.

Nunnally, J. C. (1967). *Psychometric theory.* New York: McGraw-Hill.

Yang, J. S. R. (2003). Motivational orientations and selected learner variables of East Asian language learners in the United States. *Foreign Language Annals, 36*(1), 44–56. doi: 10.1111/j.1944-9720.2003.tb01931.x

5 Wider implications and conclusions

Summary of the main findings

This book has explored stereotypes that learners of Japanese, Korean, Mandarin, Myanmar, Thai and Vietnamese languages have about the target language countries, their cultures and people. It assessed the salience of these stereotypical images and attitudes embedded in them. It then proceeded to examine associations between the language learners' country stereotypes and their L2 motivation. The findings from the content analysis of the consensual stereotypes revealed that students learning Japanese, Korean and Mandarin languages had a richer mosaic of mental images of the target language countries. It was also found that the "pictures in the head" that the learners of Mandarin, Korean and Japanese languages had of the target countries were more complete because, as the further analysis showed, more of the country-related aspects were included in the learners' mental imagery. Among the six countries, Vietnam could be described as somewhat of a *terra incognita* for the learners of Vietnamese.

Besides being mental images or "pictures in the head" *per se*, stereotypes are saturated with individual people's attitudes toward a stereotyped entity. The analysis of attitudes embedded in the language learners' mental pictures of the six target language countries allowed to conclude that, overall, the students held positive attitudes toward these countries. As the findings indicated, the composite mean valence (CompMV) values were above 0 for each country. It should be noted, however, that the difference between the most and the least positively perceived countries was considerable as the CompMV values ranged between 1.45 for Korea and Thailand and 0.68 for Myanmar. Another finding in support of the language learners' positive attitudes toward the target language countries was that, with the exception of the language learners' imagery of Myanmar, the positively rated images tended to readily come to the learners' minds and were placed at the top, or very close to the top, of their lists of images. This fact is reflected in the finding that the positive consensual stereotypes had higher salience compared to the negative ones.

Wider implications and conclusions

The empirical findings from the correlation analysis of the aggregated data for all six countries gave support to the proposition that there would exist statistically significant and positive associations between the students' mental images of the target language countries and their L2 motivation. However, in contrast to my earlier study among Malaysian learners of European languages (Nikitina, 2019), the strongest association between the country stereotypes and four components of L2 motivation was found to exist for the instrumental orientation ($r_s=.342$, $p<.01$). The association between L2 motivation and the integrative orientation, although statistically significant, was rather weak ($r_s=.217$, $p<.05$). As to the effect of the country stereotypes on L2 motivation, the results from the regression analysis of the aggregated data indicated that it was the strongest in the case of the instrumental orientation. However, the picture was more nuanced when the data for each target language country were analyzed separately. Quite unexpectedly, with the exception of Vietnam and Thailand, no strong statistically significant relationship was found to exist between the students' mental images of the target language countries and their L2 motivation.

Methodological, theoretical and pedagogical implications

Besides expanding the scope of applied linguistics research on country stereotypes to include the learners of Asian languages, this book accorded special attention to methodological and theoretical issues. (see Chapter 2 and Chapter 3). The methodological considerations were important because earlier available research on language learners' mental imagery of target language countries was, for the most part, qualitative. In contrast, L2 motivation was traditionally researched using quantitative methods and approaches. The greatest implication from adopting a mixed-methods research design is that it enabled to bridge the methodological differences and to reduce the existing research gaps. In the current book, the qualitative strand of the study explored stereotype content or mental images that language learners had of each of the six Asian countries, while the quantitative phase assessed attitudes embedded in the students' mental images and the associations between the country stereotypes and L2 motivation.

Regarding the theoretical implications, a Vygotskian concept of system of meaning with its complex architectonic that incorporates linguistic, cognitive, affective and volitional aspects involved in human psychological and speech activities could provide a propitious foundation for research on mental images of target language countries. To be more specific, the multifaceted concept of a system of meaning would allow for seamless connections between such variables as language learners' cognitive associations concerning a target language country (e.g., country images or stereotypes), their affective reactions toward the country (e.g., attitudes embedded in the mental images) and the volitional drives (e.g., L2 motivation, willingness to communicate in a foreign language) that are present in the process of learning a new language. Especially felicitous for studies in the field of applied linguistics could be theoretical approaches that employ the linguistically oriented concepts of word meaning (*znachenie slova*) and word sense (*smysl*), which form part of the Vygotskian system of meaning (Vygotsky, 1934). Chapter 2 of this book has offered a more detailed discussion as to how these two concepts could be harnessed in research on country stereotypes. In addition, I would like to propose here that the volitional aspect within the system of meaning could be approached not only from the perspective of choosing an additional language to learn and expending efforts in this endeavour (the "whys" and "therefores" of L2 motivation) but also from a broader ontological perspective of the *raison d'être* for the teaching of foreign languages. This shifts the emphasis from the internal psychological processes involved in learning an additional language to a wider plane of human endeavours and activities ("деятельность" in the widest sense), including foreign language education. This brings us to pedagogical implications of research on country stereotypes.

Researchers and language educators agree that among important objectives of any foreign language program is reducing language learners' simplistic and stereotypical perceptions of target language countries and cultures as well as enhancing the learners' awareness and appreciation of the humankind's cultural diversity (Kelly, 1969/1976; Nikitina, 2017; Schulz and Haerle, 1995). Language instructors and curriculum developers might find that knowing the content and understanding the nature of stereotypes that their students bring into the classroom could be useful when making empirically driven decisions concerning the component of the language program aimed at developing the learners' cultural awareness.

Cultural awareness in the context of foreign language education refers to the knowledge and understanding of key elements of the target culture, including the "behaviors, artifacts, ideas and values" (Ryan-Scheutz and Nuessel, 2010, p. 38). Language educators might be hesitant to introduce the language learners to values, ideas and ideals of a target culture at early stages of a language program when the students' linguistic skills are not sufficient for engagements with the target culture in the target language. As a result, the language learners are mainly exposed to information about behaviours and artifacts immanent in the target culture. Another obstacle is that the curricula prioritize, quite understandably, the development of the students' linguistic aptitude, which prepares them for examinations and tests and leaves very few affordances for explorations of the target culture. However, even at the beginner level, developing the linguistic competencies is not incompatible with enhancing cultural sensibilities, and a wide repertoire of pedagogical approaches is available for achieving the two aims simultaneously (see Abrams, 2002; Allen, 2004; Byon, 2007; Byram, 1997; Byram and Kramsch, 2008; Chaput, 1997; Nikitina, 2017; Ryan-Scheutz and Nuessel, 2010). Byram (1997), for example, has demonstrated how language learners' cross-cultural awareness could be effectively developed in tandem with their linguistic aptitude since the very beginning of a language program. His model gave much-needed legitimacy to using the language learners' mother tongue for in-depth explorations of a target culture. Byram and Kramsch (2008) and Nikitina (2017) shared some pedagogical strategies that would allow linking the teaching of target language's linguistic features with introducing learners to important cognitive categories in the target culture. Byon (2007), Allen (2004) and Abrams (2002) described how semester-long projects on a target culture implemented by language learners can help the students to verbalize, elucidate, critically assess and abandon some of their pre-conceived and false stereotypical notions.

As the present study has demonstrated, exploring the content of language learners' country stereotypes would reveal not only "what is there" and readily available in the students' mental imagery of the target language countries, but also what tends to be obscured. Identifying such lacunae could help language educators to fine-tune the cultural component of the language course to the learning needs of a particular cohort of language learners. For example, the current study's findings indicated that the teachers of Korean language might want to take note of the missing references to the traditional arts among the country images provided by the learners of Korean. They might want to provide more opportunities to their students to become better acquainted with the rich heritage of Korean arts and culture. In a similar way, quite conspicuous were the omissions by the Thai language learners of the images pertaining to the target language country's history. This gap is especially noticeable in view that Malaysia and Thailand are neighbour countries with centuries-old historical ties. In sum, there is a rich body of literature to aid language educators in their search for appropriate pedagogical strategies. What has been lacking are discussions of diverse theoretical foundations that would enable researchers to root, evolve and expand future empirical research and pedagogical practice.

Directions for future research and practice

Intellectual heritage left by Lev Vygotsky (1896–1934) could provide a solid foundation for future theoretical developments and empirical investigations in the field. The linguistically saturated concepts of word meaning (*znachenie slova*) and word sense (*smysl*) might be particularly appealing for applied linguists and foreign language educators. As with all other words people come across since their birth, by the time individual people begin learning a foreign language, they would have encountered the target language country's name (as a word, a lexical entity) in various social and cultural contexts. The influx of information about the target language country would be accompanied with, in Vygotsky's own words, the "influx of sense": the country's name in the mind of an individual language learner would have absorbed and fused the "senses" of multiple social situations, connotations, oral narratives, written texts, visuals and so on, where this particular lexical unit was encountered. Therefore, each individual language learner would have developed his or her own unique system of attitudinal and functional meanings pertaining to the target language country's name and have a range of affective responses toward it. This phenomenon is akin to what linguists describe as "semantic prosody", when otherwise neutral words would acquire either positive or negative connotations depending on their frequent co-occurrence with the obviously positive or negative words (i.e., lexical entities). Similar to semantic prosody, if a target language country happens to be depicted predominantly in the negative light in school textbooks, if it tends to receive mostly negative news coverage in the mass media and if more often than not the target language country (and its people) is portrayed as a villain, evil or an enemy in movies – and this list can go on – then, clearly, the "influx of sense" attached to the country's name would be negative.

Foreign language programs are well positioned to create multiple affordances for language learners to have more positive, meaningful and deep engagements with target cultures. A well-designed cultural component and appropriate teaching and learning activities would expand the range of educational and social contexts where the students do not encounter the country's name in a capacity of passive recipients of information but, instead, they become active participants in the creation and negotiations of the shared word meaning – the meaning(s) attached to the target language country's name. This viewpoint agrees with the Vygotskian concept of a system of meaning where cognitive, psychological, linguistic and affective components are fused in a complex architectonic.

As Chaput (1997) pointed out, "there really is no such thing as 'just language'" in foreign language teaching practice (p. 406). Developing language learners' knowledge of non-material domains of the target culture that are embedded in the target language, and therefore not readily accessible to outsiders, would result in a deeper and richer sense (*smysl*) that each individual student attaches to the word meaning *znachenie* associated with the target language country's name. Importantly, these concepts can become handy heuristic tools in using the foreign language classroom potential to create meanings that are richer, less rigid and less stereotypical compared to the ones that the students have internalized from their cultural milieus throughout the course of their life. At the same time, similar to the prior processes, each language learner would inevitably attach to the country's name his or her own "inner sense" through the workings of individual cognitive processes. The role of language educators as mediators in the processes of creating deeper, richer and more encompassing meanings associated with a lexical unit denoting a target language country cannot be overestimated.

Conclusions

Stereotypes are ubiquitous and indispensable, and for this reason they are important. Stereotypes are ever present in the foreign language classroom as students have a plethora of mental images or "pictures in the head" of target language countries, their inhabitants and cultures that they have imbibed from their social environments throughout their life. These stereotypes, if positive, might be a reason why a student chose a particular foreign language to learn and act as a powerful engine to sustain the L2 motivation. If negative, stereotypes might inhibit the outcome of the language learning endeavour. However, the main problem with stereotypes is their shallowness and reductionist nature. For this reason, foreign language educators need to raise their students' conscious awareness of the existence and the role of stereotypes in our perceptions of other countries and cultures. Moreover, a bigger mission of foreign language programs and educators is to initiate a process of deconstructing inflexible matrices consisting of stereotypes in our collective and individual consciousness and to begin creating a richer system of meaning pertaining to a target language country and the world at large. To achieve this, language educators might want to begin from exploring the content of their students' country stereotypes, especially if such knowledge is still limited, as is the case with learners of Asian languages. This book has initiated a step in this direction. Much remains to be done.

References

Abrams, Z. I. (2002). Surfing to cross-cultural awareness: Using Internet-mediated projects to explore cultural stereotypes. *Foreign Language Annals, 35*(2), 141–160.

Allen, L. Q. (2004). Implementing a culture portfolio project within a constructivist paradigm. *Foreign Language Annals, 37*(2), 232–239. doi: 10.1111/j.1944-9720.2004.tb02196.x

Byon, A. S. (2007). The use of culture portfolio project in a Korean culture classroom: Evaluating stereotypes and enhancing cross-cultural awareness. *Language, Culture and Curriculum, 20*(1), 1–19. doi: 10.2167/lcc323.0

Byram, K., & Kramsch, C. (2008). Why is it so difficult to teach language as culture? *The German Quarterly*, *81*(1), 20–34. doi: 10.2307/27676139

Byram, M. (1997). "Cultural awareness" as vocabulary learning. *The Language Learning Journal*, *16*(1), 51–57. doi: 10.1080/09571739785200291

Chaput, P. R. (1997). Culture in grammar. *The Slavic and East European Journal*, *41*(3), 403–414.

Kelly, L. G. (1969/1976). *25 centuries of language teaching*. Rowley, MA: Newbury House Publishers.

Nikitina, L. (2017). Language learners' representations of Spanish: Speaking countries: How can they inform language pedagogy? Las representaciones de los aprendices de una lengua sobre los países hablantes de español¿ Cómo pueden ellos informar sobre la pedagogía de la lengua? *Revista Signos*, *50*(93), 50–70. https://doi.org/10.4067/S0718-09342017000100003

Nikitina, L. (2019). Do country stereotypes influence language learning motivation? A study among foreign language learners in Malaysia. *Moderna Språk*, *113*(1), 58–79.

Ryan-Scheutz, C., & Nuessel, F. (2010). Teaching and assessing Italian culture in North America. *Italica*, *87*(1), 37–68. doi: 10.2307/20750677

Schulz, R. A., & Haerle, B. M. (1995). "Beer, fast cars, and . . .": Stereotypes held by U.S. college-level students of German. *Die Unterrichtspraxis/Teaching German*, *28*(1), 29–39.

Vygotsky, L. S. (1934). *Myshlenie i rech (Thinking and speech)* (in Russian). Moscow, Leningrad: Gosudarstvennoye Socialno-ekonomicheskoye Izdatel'stvo.

Appendix 1

Questionnaire on country images and L2 motivation

Dear Student,
This questionnaire explores students' mental images of Vietnam and their experiences learning the Vietnamese language. This is not an exam, and there are no "correct" or "wrong" answers. Your sincere personal opinion is the correct answer. Participation in this study is voluntary and much appreciated! Returning the filled-in questionnaire to the researcher implies your consent to participate in this study. Your answers will be treated as confidential.

Part I

1   What images or mental pictures come to your mind when you hear the words "Vietnam" or "Vietnamese"? Write as many words or short phrases as you need to in the space provided. (You can write either in English or in Malay.)

Please give a mark ranging from – 2 to +2 to each image written here. These marks should be based on your **personal opinion or attitude** toward this image.

Part II

Circle (O) or tick (√) your answer to each of the following questions. The scale is:

1 = Strongly disagree (SD); 2 = Disagree (D); 3 = Neither disagree nor agree (N); 4 = Agree (A); 5 = Strongly agree (SA)

No	Questionnaire statements	SD	D	N	A	SA
1	Knowledge of the Vietnamese language will be useful for finding a job.	1	2	3	4	5
2	Learning this language will enable me to better understand the ways of life in Vietnam.	1	2	3	4	5
3	I am working hard at learning the Vietnamese language.	1	2	3	4	5
4	Learning this language will enable me to appreciate Vietnamese art and literature.	1	2	3	4	5
5	After I complete this level of the Vietnamese language I intend to continue learning Vietnamese at a higher level.	1	2	3	4	5
6	A good proficiency in the Vietnamese language will bring me some financial benefits (e.g., translation job, etc.).	1	2	3	4	5
7	Knowledge of the Vietnamese language can be useful for my further studies, such as at the Master's or PhD level.	1	2	3	4	5
8	If my language teacher wanted someone to do an extra assignment for the class, I would certainly volunteer.	1	2	3	4	5
9	Learning Vietnamese will allow me to get to know its speakers better.	1	2	3	4	5
10	I put great efforts to understand everything my lecturer teaches us during the class.	1	2	3	4	5
11	Knowledge of the Vietnamese language will increase my job opportunities.	1	2	3	4	5
12	If the Vietnamese language was not offered in University of Malaya I would try to find Vietnamese language classes somewhere else.	1	2	3	4	5
13	I always volunteer to answer the questions my Vietnamese lecturer asks in the classroom.	1	2	3	4	5
14	Knowledge of the Vietnamese language will help me when I travel abroad.	1	2	3	4	5
15	I decided to learn this language because I am interested in Vietnamese popular culture.	1	2	3	4	5

Part III

Provide some information about yourself.

1. Gender: Male☐ Female☐
2. Age: _____ years
3. Current year of study in UM _____
4. Faculty/Institute/Academy Centre/_____

THANKS!

Appendix 2
Findings on language learners' country stereotypes

Table A4.1 Consensual stereotypes of China

No	Consensual stereotypes	Frequency (n)	Salience index (SI)	Salience rank (SR)	Mean valence (MV)	Mean valence rank (MVR)
1	Many people	8	0.228	1	−0.13	26
2	Big country	6	0.218	2	0.67	20
3	Culture	4	0.153	3	1.75	2
4	Delicious food	6	0.13	4	1.67	3
5	Communism	4	0.129	5	−0.50	28
6	Technology	7	0.122	6	1.57	6
7	History	3	0.085	7	1.33	15
8	Advanced country	3	0.068	8	1.33	15
9	5000 years of history	2	0.065	9	1.00	17
10	Mystery	3	0.059	10	1.67	3
11	Strong country	3	0.055	11	0.67	20
12	Smart	3	0.051	12	1.67	3
13	*Beijing*	2	0.05	13	1.50	7
14	Poetry	2	0.05	13	1.50	7
15	Unfriendly	2	0.05	13	−1.00	29
16	Modern country	2	0.048	16	1.50	7
17	*Xi Jinping*	2	0.047	17	0.00	23
18	Economy	2	0.044	18	1.50	7
19	*Great Wall*	2	0.043	19	1.50	7
20	Complex	2	0.04	20	1.50	7
21	Developed country	3	0.038	21	1.00	17
22	Fast-paced country	2	0.036	22	0.00	23
23	Hardworking	2	0.033	23	1.00	17
24	Tea	2	0.032	24	1.50	7

No	Consensual stereotypes	Frequency (n)	Salience index (SI)	Salience rank (SR)	Mean valence (MV)	Mean valence rank (MVR)
25	Weibo	2	0.032	24	1.50	7
26	Rich	2	0.031	26	0.50	22
27	Patriotic	2	0.027	27	0.00	23
28	Chinese literature	2	0.023	28	2.00	1
29	Selfish	2	0.021	29	−1.50	30
30	Difficult to learn language	3	0.016	30	−0.33	27

Note: Unique stereotypes of China are typed in italics.

Table A4.2 Categories of images of China

Category	Number of images	Mean valence (MV)	Mean valence rank (MVR)	Salience index (SI)	Salience rank (SR)
Mysterious and complex country	4	1.75	1	0.078	13
Cuisine and food	10	1.70	2	0.132	9
Literature and poetry	5	1.60	3	0.049	14
Technology	7	1.57	4	0.122	11
Traditional culture and culture symbols	15	1.40	5	0.245	2
Social media and e-commerce	8	1.25	6	0.038	15
History	9	1.22	7	0.233	3
Advanced and developed country	10	1.10	8	0.152	6
Cities, places and sites	10	0.90	9	0.113	12
Modern, fast-paced and strong country	7	0.71	10	0.14	8
Big country	6	0.67	11	0.218	5
Language	6	0.67	11	0.13	10
People	38	0.32	13	0.265	1
Large population	8	−0.13	14	0.228	4
Political system and international position	8	−0.63	15	0.147	7
Others	10				
Total	**161**				
Composite mean valence (CompMV)		0.86			

Note: Images in the category "Others" were aggregated in the calculation of the total number of images and computation of the composite mean valence (CompMV).

Table A4.3 Consensual stereotypes of Japan

No	Consensual stereotypes	Frequency (n)	Salience index (SI)	Salience rank (SR)	Mean valence (MV)	Mean valence rank (MVR)
1	Sushi	3	0.402	1	1.67	9
2	Sakura	3	0.344	2	1.67	9
3	Anime	3	0.334	3	0.33	30
4	Kimono	3	0.264	4	1.33	20
5	Yukata	2	0.163	5	1.50	13
6	Ageing society	4	0.129	6	−1.75	37
7	Tokyo	4	0.129	6	1.50	13
8	Samurai	4	0.128	8	1.00	21
9	Cleanliness	4	0.12	9	2.00	1
10	Takoyaki	3	0.116	10	1.00	21
11	Akihabara	2	0.109	11	2.00	1
12	Tea ceremony	2	0.108	12	1.50	13
13	Shinkansen	2	0.106	13	1.50	13
14	Discipline	2	0.104	14	1.50	13
15	Mount Fuji	3	0.095	15	2.00	1
16	Sashimi	2	0.094	16	0.50	27
17	Manga	3	0.085	17	0.33	30
18	Ramen	2	0.082	18	1.00	21
19	Manners	3	0.074	19	1.67	9
20	Natto	2	0.074	19	0.00	33
21	Summer festival	2	0.065	21	2.00	1
22	Shrine	3	0.063	22	1.67	9
23	Toyota	2	0.062	23	2.00	1
24	Shibuya	2	0.061	24	0.00	33
25	Technology	2	0.059	25	1.50	13
26	Kanji	3	0.058	26	0.33	30
27	Uniqlo	2	0.055	27	0.50	27
28	Tsunami	2	0.047	28	−1.50	36
29	Wasabi	2	0.046	29	2.00	1
30	J-pop	2	0.039	30	−0.50	35
31	Nuclear power plant	2	0.039	30	−2.00	38
32	Economy	3	0.037	32	2.00	1
33	Lawson	2	0.028	33	1.00	21
34	Seaweed	2	0.025	34	1.00	21
35	Cosplay	2	0.024	35	1.00	21
36	Ninja	2	0.023	36	1.50	13
37	Katakana	2	0.016	37	0.50	27
38	Low crime rate	2	0.008	38	2.00	1

Note: Unique stereotypes of Japan are typed in italics.

Table A4.4 Categories of images of Japan

Category	Number of images	Mean valence (MV)	Mean valence rank (MVR)	Salience index (SI)	Salience rank (SR)
Modern lifestyle	5	2.00	1	0.127	10
Seasons	2	2.00	1	0.045	14
Economy	3	2.00	1	0.037	15
People	9	1.89	4	0.173	7
Technology and car makers	11	1.82	5	0.187	6
Social values	10	1.60	6	0.202	5
Traditional culture and culture symbols	30	1.53	7	0.534	2
Cities, places and sites	19	1.53	7	0.285	4
Food and beverages	36	1.33	9	0.541	1
Brands	8	1.13	10	0.099	12
Language	9	0.78	11	0.153	8
Pop culture	21	0.43	12	0.395	3
History	5	0.20	13	0.111	11
Natural and man-made disasters	6	−1.67	14	0.089	13
Society issues	10	−1.70	15	0.144	9
Other	1				
Total images*	**185**				
Composite mean valence (CompMV)		**1.24**			

Note: Images in the category "Others" were aggregated in the calculation of the total number of images and computation of the composite mean valence (CompMV).

Table A4.5 Consensual stereotypes of Korea

No	Consensual stereotypes	Frequency (n)	Salience index (SI)	Salience rank (SR)	Mean valence (MV)	Mean valence rank (MVR)
1	K-pop	6	0.821	1	1.33	26
2	K-dramas	12	0.355	2	1.42	25
3	Kimchi	3	0.317	3	1.00	30
4	Hanbok	3	0.217	4	1.67	6
5	Kimbap	3	0.16	5	1.33	26
6	Samsung	3	0.136	6	1.00	30
7	Annyeonghaseyo	3	0.126	7	2.00	1

(*Continued*)

Table A4.5 (Continued)

No	Consensual stereotypes	Frequency (n)	Salience index (SI)	Salience rank (SR)	Mean valence (MV)	Mean valence rank (MVR)
8	*Jeju Island*	4	0.11	8	1.75	5
9	*Hangul*	4	0.105	9	1.50	8
10	Fashion	2	0.104	10	1.50	8
11	*Saranghae*	3	0.097	11	1.33	26
12	*Oppa*	2	0.096	12	1.50	8
13	*Bibimbap*	2	0.088	13	1.50	8
14	*Namsan Tower*	3	0.084	14	0.67	33
15	*Sejong the Great*	3	0.083	15	1.33	26
16	*Park Geun-hye*	4	0.08	16	−0.25	36
17	Plastic surgery	2	0.075	17	−0.50	37
18	*Winter Sonata*	2	0.067	18	1.50	8
19	Food	2	0.065	19	2.00	1
20	Cosmetics	2	0.063	20	1.50	8
21	*Ramyeon*	3	0.059	21	1.67	6
22	Safe	2	0.057	22	2.00	1
23	*Running Man*	2	0.053	23	1.50	8
24	"Gangnam Style"	2	0.05	24	1.50	8
25	*Han River*	2	0.043	25	1.50	8
26	*Ppali-ppali culture*	3	0.042	26	1.00	30
27	*Country divided into two*	2	0.042	26	0.50	34
28	*Seoul*	2	0.041	28	1.50	8
29	*SM Entertainment*	2	0.038	29	1.50	8
30	Makeup	2	0.032	30	1.50	8
31	Subway	2	0.032	30	1.50	8
32	*Nami Island*	2	0.031	32	1.50	8
33	*Big Bang*	2	0.029	33	0.50	34
34	*Busan*	2	0.028	34	1.50	8
35	*Korean food*	2	0.027	35	1.50	8
36	*Kamsahamnida*	2	0.017	36	1.50	8
37	Olympic games	2	0.007	37	2.00	1

Note: Unique stereotypes of Korea are typed in italics.

Table A4.6 Categories of images of Korea

Category	Number of images	Mean valence (MV)	Mean valence rank (MVR)	Salience index (SI)	Salience rank (SR)
Affective reaction	3	1.67	1	0.076	12
History	5	1.60	2	0.121	11
Food	25	1.56	3	0.482	2
Traditional culture	11	1.55	4	0.351	3
K-pop, K-drama and entertainment	42	1.52	5	0.715	1

Category	Number of images	Mean valence (MV)	Mean valence rank (MVR)	Salience index (SI)	Salience rank (SR)
Language	14	1.50	6	0.214	7
Fashion and cosmetics	6	1.50	6	0.134	8
Economy and technology	5	1.40	8	0.129	9
Cities, geographical names and sites	19	1.37	9	0.227	5
Brands	6	1.33	10	0.128	10
Modern society and lifestyle	25	1.16	11	0.264	4
People	18	1.11	12	0.216	6
Divided country	5	0.00	13	0.059	13
Others	4				
Total images*	**188**				
Composite mean valence (CompMV)		**1.45**			

Note: Images in the category "Others" were aggregated in the calculation of the total number of images and computation of the composite mean valence (CompMV).

Table A4.7 Consensual stereotypes of Myanmar

No	Consensual stereotypes	Frequency (n)	Salience index (SI)	Salience rank (SR)	Mean valence (MV)	Mean valence rank (MVR)
1	Rich culture	8	0.292	1	1.75	3
2	South East Asian country	4	0.211	2	1.25	10
3	Buddhist country	5	0.21	3	1.60	6
4	Ethnic problems	4	0.2	4	−2.00	17
5	*Rohingya people*	5	0.192	5	−1.00	15
6	Interesting language	4	0.128	6	1.75	3
7	Country near China and India	4	0.126	7	0.25	14
8	Big country	4	0.123	8	1.25	10
9	*Burmese history*	4	0.109	9	1.50	7
10	Traditional clothes	4	0.104	10	2.00	1
11	*Thanaka*	2	0.086	11	1.00	12
12	Pagodas	4	0.078	12	1.75	3

(*Continued*)

Table A4.7 (Continued)

No	Consensual stereotypes	Frequency (n)	Salience index (SI)	Salience rank (SR)	Mean valence (MV)	Mean valence rank (MVR)
13	Many ethnic groups	2	0.062	13	1.50	7
14	*Aung San Suu Kyi*	3	0.06	14	1.33	9
15	Lack of modern facilities	2	0.05	15	−2.00	17
16	Military government	2	0.035	16	−2.00	17
17	Festivals	2	0.032	17	2.00	1
18	Large population	2	0.024	18	0.50	13
19	Not a well-known country	2	0.02	19	−1.50	16

Note: Unique stereotypes of Myanmar are typed in italics.

Table A4.8 Categories of images of Myanmar

Category	Number of images	Mean valence (MV)	Mean valence rank (MVR)	Salience index (SI)	Salience rank (SR)
Culture and history	23	1.65	1	0.418	2
Religion and religious sites	13	1.46	2	0.233	5
Language	14	1.36	3	0.3	4
Country location, country size and standing	20	0.60	4	0.409	3
People and population	13	0.38	5	0.181	6
Multi-ethnic country, ethnic issues, political situation	21	−0.81	6	0.479	1
Economy, lack of technology	8	−1.13	7	0.121	7
Others	14				
Total images*	**126**				
Composite mean valence (CompMV)		0.68			

Note: Images in the category "Others" were aggregated in the calculation of the total number of images and computation of the composite mean valence (CompMV).

Table A4.9 Consensual stereotypes of Thailand

No	Consensual stereotypes	Frequency (n)	Salience index (SI)	Salience rank (SR)	Mean valence (MV)	Mean valence rank (MVR)
1	Tom yam	6	0.379	1	1.67	13
2	Food	7	0.355	2	2.00	1
3	Thai movies	7	0.213	3	2.00	1
4	Krabi	5	0.203	4	1.60	15
5	Muay Thai	5	0.181	5	0.80	33
6	Places to visit	5	0.163	6	1.80	9
7	Bangkok	4	0.162	7	1.00	30
8	Beautiful people	7	0.156	8	1.57	16
9	Horror movies	5	0.139	9	1.20	29
10	Soft language	4	0.133	10	1.50	17
11	Friendly people	5	0.118	11	1.80	9
12	Sawasdee	3	0.114	12	2.00	1
13	Som tam	4	0.109	13	1.75	11
14	Hat Yai	2	0.109	13	1.50	17
15	Thai songs	4	0.097	15	1.50	17
16	Handsome actors	4	0.096	16	1.75	11
17	Festivals	3	0.084	17	2.00	1
18	Massage	4	0.078	18	1.50	17
19	Interesting language	3	0.073	19	1.33	26
20	Thai people	2	0.066	20	2.00	1
21	Beautiful islands	3	0.066	20	1.33	26
22	Shopping	4	0.063	22	1.25	28
23	Thai culture	2	0.061	23	1.50	17
24	Thai language	3	0.059	24	1.67	13
25	Water festival	2	0.059	24	0.50	34
26	Thai script	2	0.058	26	1.50	17
27	Market on boats	2	0.053	27	1.00	30
28	Nice people	2	0.052	28	1.50	17
29	Loyalty to their king	2	0.048	29	2.00	1
30	Politeness	2	0.048	29	1.50	17
31	Beautiful scenery	2	0.045	31	1.00	30
32	Pondan (transvestite)	3	0.036	32	−1.33	35
33	Actors	2	0.028	33	2.00	1
34	Beaches	2	0.027	34	2.00	1
35	War	2	0.024	35	−2.00	36
36	Elephants	2	0.022	36	1.50	17

Note: Unique stereotypes of Thailand are typed in italics.

Table A4.10 Categories of images of Thailand

Category	Number of images	Mean valence (MV)	Mean valence rank (MVR)	Salience index (SI)	Salience rank (SR)
Food	20	1.80	1	0.497	2
Beautiful islands, beaches, sea	13	1.62	2	0.301	6
Popular culture	17	1.59	3	0.321	5
Language	18	1.56	4	0.294	7
People	30	1.53	5	0.373	3
Cities, sites, places to visit	18	1.44	6	0.35	4
Traditional culture, cultural symbols, religion	25	1.20	7	0.513	1
Contemporary lifestyle and society	21	0.95	8	0.15	8
Country descriptions	11	0.91	9	0.087	9
Others	4				
Total images*	**177**				
Composite mean valence (CompMV)		**1.45**			

Note: Images in the category "Others" were aggregated in the calculation of the total number of images and computation of the composite mean valence (CompMV).

Table A4.11 Consensual stereotypes of Vietnam

No	Consensual stereotypes	Frequency	Salience index (SI)	Salience rank (SR)	Mean valence (MV)	Mean valence rank (MVR)
1	*Ho Chi Minh city*	4	0.424	1	1.25	3
2	*Hanoi*	3	0.282	2	0.67	6
3	*Vietnam war*	4	0.207	3	−0.50	7
4	*Vietnamese food*	4	0.182	4	0.75	5
5	Communism	3	0.115	5	−0.67	8
6	Traditional outfit	4	0.11	6	1.50	1
7	Easy language	4	0.064	7	1.25	3
8	Water puppets	2	0.051	8	1.50	1

Note: Unique stereotypes of Vietnam are typed in italics.

Table A4.12 Categories of images of Vietnam

Category	Number of images (n)	Mean valence (MV)	Mean valence rank (MVR)	Salience index (SI)	Salience rank (SR)
Weather and seasons	3	2.00	1	0.056	10
Language	17	1.65	2	0.309	2
Culture and ways of life	12	1.08	3	0.274	3
Cities	8	1.00	4	0.421	1
People	11	1.00	4	0.161	8
Economy	3	1.00	4	0.086	9
Food	4	0.75	7	0.182	6
History	5	0.20	8	0.236	4
Political system	4	−0.50	9	0.192	5
China's influence	4	−0.50	9	0.173	7
Other	5				
Total images*	**76**				
Composite mean valence (CompMV)		**1.04**			

Note: Images in the category "Others" were aggregated in the calculation of the total number of images and computation of the composite mean valence (CompMV).

Table A4.13 Findings from the EFA

Questionnaire items and variables	Factors			
	1	2	3	4
	Inst	Integ	Pers	Effort
Knowledge of the Japanese language will increase my job opportunities (Inst)*	.809			
Learning the Japanese language will allow me to get to know its speakers better (Integ)	.694			
Knowledge of the Japanese language will be useful for finding a job (Inst)	.689			
Knowledge of the Japanese language will help me when I travel abroad (Inst)	.595			
Being proficient in the Japanese language will bring me some financial benefits (e.g., translation jobs, etc.) (Inst)	.593			
Knowledge of the Japanese language can be useful for my further studies, such as at the Master's or PhD level (Inst)	.505			
I am working hard at learning the Japanese language (Gen)		.758		

(*Continued*)

Table A4.13 (Continued)

Questionnaire items and variables	Factors			
	1 Inst	2 Integ	3 Pers	4 Effort
Learning this language will enable me to appreciate Japanese art and literature (Integ)		.754		
I decided to learn this language because I am interested in Japanese popular culture (Integ)		.587		
If the Japanese language was not offered in the University of Malaya I would try to find Japanese language classes somewhere else (Gen)			.742	
If my language teacher wanted someone to do an extra assignment for the class, I would certainly volunteer (Gen)			.707	
After I complete this Level 1 of the Japanese language I intend to continue learning Japanese at a higher level (Gen)			.476	
I always volunteer to answer the questions my Japanese language teacher asks in the classroom (Gen)				.733
Learning this language will enable me to better understand the ways of life in Japan (Integ)				.641
I put great efforts to understand everything my language instructor teaches us during the class (Gen)				.459
Cronbach's alpha	.786	.641	.667	.550

Notes: Extraction method was the Principal Component Analysis; only loadings above .450 are shown.

* Variables: Ins=Instrumental orientation; Integ=Integrative orientation; Gen=General motivation; Pers=Perseverance

Table A4.14 Findings from the Spearman rank correlation test on the relationships between the language learners' country images and L2 motivation (data aggregated for all six countries)

Variables	1	2	3	4	5
1 Instrumental orientation					
2 Integrative orientation	.418**				
3 Perseverance	.462**	.459**			
4 Effort	.457**	.386**	.463**		
5 Stereotypes	.342**	.217*	.337**	.189*	

** Indicates statistical significance at the 1 percent level.
* Indicates statistical significance at the 5 percent level.

Table A4.15 Findings from the Spearman rank correlation test on the relationships between the language learners' country images and L2 motivation (data for each target language country)

Country	Instrumental orientation	Integrative orientation	Perseverance	Effort
China	.266	.276	.284	.240
Japan	.237	.069	.402	.294
Korea	.022	.269	.280	−.063
Myanmar	.193	.112	−.090	.121
Thailand	.403	.026	.464*	.068
Vietnam	.622*	.605*	.575*	.263

* Indicates statistical significance at the 5 percent level.

Table A4.16 Findings from the robust multiple regression analysis

Independent variable	Dependent variable (L2 motivation)							
	Instrumental orientation		Integrative orientation		Perseverance		Effort	
	β	t	β	t	β	t	β	t
Stereotypes	.362	4.398	.289	3.415	.352	4.253	.255	2.987
R^2	.131		.083		.124		.065	
95% CI	[0.261; 0.355]		[0.249; 0.368]		[0.351; 0.485]		[0.185; 0.268]	

Notes: β is a standardized regression coefficient; t is t-statistic; R^2 is the coefficient of determination; CI is the confidence interval.

Appendix 3
SPSS codes for the regression analysis[1]

matrix.
get x/ variable x1.
get y/ variable y1.
compute n=nrow(y).
compute cons=make(n,1,1).
compute x={x,cons}.
compute tx=transpos(x).
compute invx=inv(tx*x).
compute xy=tx*y.
compute b=invx*xy.
print b.
compute e=y-x*b.
compute te=transpos(e).
compute ee=te*e.
compute ee=diag(ee).
compute ee=csum(ee).
compute df1=nrow(x).
compute df2=ncol(x).
compute df=df1-df2.
compute ss=ee/df.
compute sd=sqrt(diag(ss*invx)).
print sd.
compute tt=b&/sd.
print tt.
end matrix.

SPSS code for regression a loop

matrix.
get x1/ variable x1.
get y1/ variable y1.
get x2/ variable x2.

```
get y2/ variable y2.
get x3/ variable x3.
get y3/ variable y3.
get x4/ variable x4.
get y4/ variable y4.

loop #s=1 to 4.
do if (#s=1).
compute x=x1.
compute y=y1.
else if (#s=2).
compute x=x2.
compute y=y2.
else if (#s=3).
compute x=x3.
compute y=y3.
else if (#s=4).
compute x=x4.
compute y=y4.
end if.

compute n=nrow(y).
compute cons=make(n,1,1).
compute x={x,cons}.
compute tx=transpos(x).
compute invx=inv(tx*x).
compute xy=tx*y.
compute b=invx*xy.
print b.
compute e=y-x*b.
compute te=transpos(e).
compute ee=te*e.
compute ee=diag(ee).
compute ee=csum(ee).
compute df1=nrow(x).
compute df2=ncol(x).
compute df=df1-df2.
compute ss=ee/df.
compute sd=sqrt(diag(ss*invx)).
print sd.
compute tt=b&/sd.
print tt.

end loop.
end matrix.
exe.
```

Appendix 3

SPSS codes for bootstrapped regression

set mxloops=1000.
save outfile 'output.sav'.
matrix.
get x1/ variable indmv.
get x2/ variable indmv.
get x3/ variable indmv.
get x4/ variable indmv.
get y1/ variable instrum.
get y2/ variable integr.
get y3/ variable pers.
get y4/ variable eff.
* number of repetition.
compute nc=make(1,1,1).
compute nc(1)=1000.
* number of independent variables.
compute nd=make(1,1,1).
compute nd(1)=4.
compute pp=make(nc(1),1,1).
* number of cases.
compute nk=make(1,1,1).
compute nk(1)=20.

loop #q=1 to nd(1).
do if (#q=1).
compute xx=x1.
compute yy=y1.
compute x0=x1.
compute y0=y1.
else if (#q=2).
compute xx=x2.
compute yy=y2.
compute x0=x2.
compute y0=y2.
else if (#q=3).
compute xx=x3.
compute yy=y3.
compute x0=x3.
compute y0=y3.
else if (#q=4).
compute xx=x4.
compute yy=y4.
compute x0=x4.

compute y0=y4.
end if.
loop #d=1 to nc(1).
compute nn=nrow(y1).
compute boot11=uniform(nn,1).
compute nnm=make(nn,1,nn).
compute boot12=boot11&*nnm.
compute boot1=trunc(boot12)+1.
compute boot21=uniform(nn,1).
compute nnm=make(nn,1,nn).
compute boot22=boot21&*nnm.
compute boot2=trunc(boot22)+1.

loop #z=1 to nk(1).
 loop #k=1 to nk(1).
  do if (boot1(#k)=#z).
   do if (#q=1).
    compute xx(#z)=x1(#k).
   else if (#q=2).
    compute xx(#z)=x2(#k).
   else if (#q=3).
    compute xx(#z)=x3(#k).
   else if (#q=4).
    compute xx(#z)=x4(#k).
   end if.
  end if.
 end loop.
end loop.

loop #a=1 to nk(1).
 loop #b=1 to nk(1).
  do if (boot2(#b)=#a).
   do if (#q=1).
    compute yy(#a)=y1(#b).
   else if (#q=2).
    compute yy(#a)=y2(#b).
   else if (#q=3).
    compute yy(#a)=y3(#b).
   else if (#q=4).
    compute yy(#a)=y4(#b).
   end if.
  end if.
 end loop.
end loop.

Appendix 3

```
do if (#d=1).
compute x=x0.
compute y=y0.
Else.
compute x=xx.
compute y=yy.
end if.
compute n=nrow(y).
compute cons=make(n,1,1).
compute x={x,cons}.
compute tx=transpos(x).
compute invx=inv(tx*x).
compute xy=tx*y.
compute b=invx*xy.
compute e=y-x*b.
compute te=transpos(e).
compute ee=te*e.
compute ee=diag(ee).
compute ee=csum(ee).
compute df1=nrow(x).
compute df2=ncol(x).
compute df=df1-df2.
compute ss=ee/df.
compute sd=sqrt(diag(ss*invx)).
compute tt=b&/sd.
compute pp(#d)=b(1).
do if (#d=1).
compute b1=b(1).
compute sd1=sd(1).
compute tt1=tt(1).
end if.
*#d, number of repetition.
end loop.
    compute pps=grade(pp).
    loop #h=1 to nc(1).
    do if (pps(#h)=995).
    compute ci99_up1=pp(#h).
    compute ci99_up=b1*2-ci99_up1.
    else if (pps(#h)=5).
    compute ci99_lo1=pp(#h).
    compute ci99_lo=b1*2-ci99_lo1.
```

```
else if (pps(#h)=975).
  compute ci95_up1=pp(#h).
  compute ci95_up=b1*2-ci95_up1.
else if (pps(#h)=25).
  compute ci95_lo1=pp(#h).
  compute ci95_lo=b1*2-ci95_lo1.
else if (pps(#h)=950).
  compute ci90_up1=pp(#h).
  compute ci90_up=b1*2-ci90_up1.
else if (pps(#h)=50).
  compute ci90_lo1=pp(#h).
  compute ci90_lo=b1*2-ci90_lo1.
end if.
end loop.

print b1.
print sd1.
print tt1.

print ci99_up.
print ci99_lo.
print ci95_up.
print ci95_lo.
print ci90_up.
print ci90_lo.

save {pp} /outfile='output.sav'.

*#q, 1, x1.
end loop.

end matrix.
exe.
```

Note

1 I would like to thank Fumitaka Furuoka for developing the codes.

Glossary

Attitude is a language learner's favourable or unfavourable disposition toward a target language country, its cultures and people. In this study the attitude is quantitatively measured by the valence ratings assigned by each student to his or her list of images of a target language country.

Composite mean valence (CompMV) is the sum total of valence ratings given to all images of a target language country divided by the number of these images.

Consensual stereotype is a stereotype or mental image shared by two or more learners of an Asian language.

Favourability. See "Valence".

Individual list is a list of images of a target language country generated by each individual student who participated in this study. The word "list" is used interchangeably with the term "inventory".

Instrumental orientation is a language learner's intention to learn a target language for practical purposes, such as getting financial benefits, employment or study opportunities.

Integrative orientation is a student's intention to learn a target language for purposes of communicating with speakers of this language and gaining a better understanding of a target language country, its cultures, its people and their ways of life.

Mean valence (MV) is the sum total of valence ratings given to all images in a group (e.g., consensual stereotypes or category of images) divided by the number of images in this group.

Motivation (or L2 motivation) is effort and perseverance that a language learner is willing to expend to learn a target language to achieve his or her goals plus a favourable interest in positive attitudes toward a target language country, its cultures, its people and the language itself.

Salience is the prominence or importance of a stereotypical image or group of images. Its calculation is based on the position of an image in the individual lists of images.

Salience index (SI) is a numerical value that indicates the prominence or salience of a stereotypical image or category of images. The index rages between 0 and 1.

Stereotype is a mental image of a target language country, its cultures and its people held by language learners. The terms "stereotypes", "stereotypical images", "country stereotypes" and "mental images" are used interchangeably in this book.

Stereotype content is all mental images of a target language country, its cultures and its people provided by students.

Target language is a specific foreign language, such as Japanese, Korean, Mandarin, Myanmar, Thai or Vietnamese, that is learned by a student or a group of students in this study.

Target language country is a country where a specific target language is spoken.

Valence is the direction and strength of a language learner's attitude. Valence can be positive, negative or neutral.

Valence rating is a numerical number assigned by a student to each image of a target language country in his or her individual list of images. The ratings in this study ranged from -2 to $+2$.

Index

Note: Page numbers in *italics* indicate figures and in **bold** indicate tables on the corresponding pages.

Abrams, Z. I. 19, 20, 22, 91, 93
accuracy of stereotypes 7, 11–13, 48
Allen, L. Q. 19, 20, 22, 91, 93
Allport, G. 6
applied linguistics research: construct of attitude in psychology and 31–33; and contributions to scholarship on stereotypes 34–36; country stereotypes and 19–21, 89–91; directions for future research and practice in 91–93; motivation in 26–30
Aron, A. 51, 52, 86
Aron, E. 51, 52, 86
attitude: applied linguistics research on 32–33; assessment 20, connecting the dots between stereotypes, L2 motivation and 33–36; embedded in mental images 8, 14, 17, 21, 50, 83, 88; etymology and definitions of 31–32, 116; as research variable 30, 84; valence and 18, 52, 117
Attitudes and Motivation in Second Language Learning (Gardner and Lambert) 21

Banaji, M. R. 13, 14, 33
Bar-Tal, D. 10, 11, 14
Benedict, R. 5
Blum, L. 13–14
Boo, Z. 42
Boulding, K. E. 11
Braly, K. W. 6, 11, 13, 15, 17, 16, 23

Byon, A. S. 30, 34, 91
Byram, K. 19, 91
Byram, M. 91

categories of images: of China 56–59, 99; of Japan 60–64, **101**; of Korea 66–69, **102–103**; of Myanmar 70–73, **104**; of Thailand 74–76, **106**; of Vietnam 77–79, **107**
Chaiken, S. 31
Chaput, P. R. 19, 22, 27, 32, 37, 92
check-lists 15–16
China, mental images of 55–59; categories of images of **98**; consensual stereotypes of **98–99**; findings on 79–83, **80, 81**; summary of main findings on 88–89
Clark, T. 5
closed-ended items 15, 16, 21, 41, 42, 43–44, 50
coding process in mixed-methods approach 47–48
Cohen, J. 52
composite mean valence (CompMV) 48, 80, 83, 88; calculation of 49; definition of 116
consensual stereotypes 13–14; definition of 116; of China 55–56 **98–99**; of Japan 60, **100**; of Korea 64–66, **101–102**; of Myanmar 70, **103–104**; of Thailand 73–74, **105**; of Vietnam 76–77, **106**

content analysis in mixed-methods approach 41, 45–46
correlation analysis 52, 84, 86, 89; findings from **108**, **109**
country stereotypes 8, 89–91; mixed-methods approach to (*see* mixed-methods approach); *see also* mental images
Cronbach's alpha 50, 51, 84; findings on **108**
Csizér, K. 29–30, 32, 83

Deci, E. L. 26, 28
De Luca Braun, R. 10
Dörnyei, Z. 26, 27, 29–30, 33, 42, 44, 51
Drewelow, I. 20, 34, 42

Eagly, A. H. 31
Echtner, C. M. 8, 12, 48, 80
Ehrlich, H. J. 15–16
exploratory factor analysis (EFA) 50, 50–51, 84; findings from **107–108**
external stereotype formation 9–11

formation of stereotypes 9–11
free-response technique 16–17
free-lists 46
Furbee, L. 16, 48, 54
Furuoka, F. 12, 18, 19, 20, 52, 82, 115

Gardner, R. C. 13, 19, 21, 26–29, 30, 32, 37, 42, 83
goal setting in language learning 28–30

Haerle, B. M. 13, 19, 20, 32, 42, 90
Hair, J. F. *et al.* 51, 52
Heinzmann, S. 2, 19, 20, 21, 30, 34

instrumental orientation 28–30; definitions of 26, 29, 116; measurement of 44
integrative orientation 28–30; definitions of 26, 29, 116; measurement of 44
internal stereotype formation 9–11

Japan, mental images of 59–64; categories of images of **101**; consensual stereotypes of **100**;

Index 119

findings on 79–83, **80**, **81**; summary of main findings on 88–89
Jones, J. M. 7, 17

Katz, D. 6, 11, 13, 15, 16
Katz–Braly list 17
Klineberg, O. 9, 35
Korea, mental images of 64–69; categories of images of **102–103**; consensual stereotypes of **101–102**; findings on 79–83, **80**, **81**; summary of main findings on 88–89
Kormos, J. 30, 32, 83
Kramsch, C. 19, 34, 91

L2 motivation 2, 26–28; definitions of 28, 116; goal setting and 29–30; mental images and 84–86; mixed-methods approach to (*see* mixed-methods approach); stereotypes, attitudes, and 33–36
L2 Motivational Self System (L2MSS) framework 27
language attitudes 30, 34
Lambert, W. E. 9, 19, 21, 26, 28, 30, 32, 35, 42, 83
Leerssen, J. 11–12
Lindsay, I. 12, 13
Lippmann, W. 1, 4–5, 7, 8, 10, 13, 17, 31, 33, 35

Mackie, D. M. 8
Mackie, M.M. 7
Maynard, K. 16, 48, 54
mean valence (MV) *41*; calculation of 49; definition of 116
mental images: attitudes embedded in 83; of China 55–59; findings on 79–83, **80**, **81**; of Japan 59–64; of Korea 64–69; of Myanmar 69–73; stereotypes, L2 motivation and 84–86; summary of main findings on 88–89; of Thailand 73–76; of Vietnam 76–79
Messick, D. M. 8
mixed-methods approach: aim, research questions, and research design 40, *41*; analysis of qualitative data in 45–48; analysis of quantitative data in 48–52; data collection and

organization in 45; need for 42–43; research instrument in 43–44; sampling method and participants in 44–45
motivation (see also L2 motivation): definition of 116
motivation in applied linguistics research 26–30
Myanmar, mental images of 69–73; categories of images of **104**; consensual stereotypes of **103–104**; findings on 79–83, **80**, **81**; summary of main findings on 88–89

national stereotypes 2, 6, 8, 9, 11, 12, 17, 20, 21, 42
Nikitina, L. 2, 6, 8, 12, 18, 19, 20, 28, 29, 30, 32, 34, 42, 43, 52, 82, 83, 84, 86, 89, 90, 91
Nunnally, J. C. 51, 86

open-ended questions 15, 34, 41, 42, 43
Oppenheim, A. N. 32
Oskamp, S. 7, 31, 32

Patterns of Culture (Benedict) 5
Piaget, J. 9, 10, 35
Public Opinion (Lippmann) 4

Quick, S. 16, 48, 54

regression analysis 50, 52, 85, 86, 89; findings from **109**
reliability analysis 50, 51
Rinehart, J. W. 15–16
Ritchie, J. R. B. 8, 12, 48, 80
Robins, R. W. 11
Ross, L. 16, 48, 54
Ryan, R. M. 26, 28, 42

salience: definition of 117; of stereotypes 3, 16, 17–18, 20, 36, 41, 48
Salience Index (SI) xiii, 41, 46, 48, 117; definition of 117
sampling method 44–45
Schneider, D. J. 6–7, 14
Schultz, P. W. 7, 31, 32
Schulz, R. A. 13, 19, 20, 32, 42, 90

Scott, W. A. 31
Shaheen, J. G. 10
Skubikowski, U. 10
Smith, J. J. 16, 48, 54
Spearman's correlation test 52; finding from **108**, **109**
Spencer-Rodgers, J. 6, 8, 13, 14, 15, 16, 17, 18, 49
stereotypes 1–2; accuracy of 11–13, 48; in applied linguistics 19–21; applied linguistics research contributing to scholarship on 34–36; consensual 13–14, 55–56, 60, 64–66, 70, 73–74, 76–77; content of 8, 15, 17, 20, 117; country and national 8, 89–91 (*see also* mental images); as culturally salient entities 13–14; definitions of 6–7, 117; individual 13–14; as interdisciplinary construct 5–6; individual *vs* consensual 14–15; internal and external processes in formation of 9–11; issues in research on 6–14; language learners' country 84–86; linkages between attitudes, L2 motivation and 33–36; measuring 17–18; mixed-methods approaches to research on (*see* mixed-methods approach); origins of the construct of 4–5; overview of methodological approaches in research on 14–18; valence and salience of 17–18
stereotype content 15, 41; findings on 79–83; structured approaches in research on 14, 15–16; unstructured approaches in research on 14, 15, 16–17

target language: definition of 117
target language country: definition of 117
Taylor, I. C. 19, 20, 34
Thailand, mental images of 73–76; categories of images of **106**; consensual stereotypes of **105**; findings on 79–83, **80**, **81**; summary of main findings on 88–89

valence 18, 46, 52; analysis of 48–49;
definitions of 18, 117; of stereotypes
17–18
valence ratings 18, 48; definition of 117
Vietnam, mental images of 76–79;
categories of images of **107**;
consensual stereotypes of **106**;
findings on 79–83, **80**, **81**; summary
of main findings on 88–89

Vygotsky, L. i, 11, 33, 34–35, 42, 90, 91–92
Weil, A. M. 9, 10, 24, 35
word meaning (*znachenie slova*) i, 2, 21, 34–35, 42, 90, 91
word sense (*smysl*) i, 2, 3, 21, 35, 42, 90, 91
World War II 5–6, 64

For Product Safety Concerns and Information please contact our EU representative GPSR@taylorandfrancis.com
Taylor & Francis Verlag GmbH, Kaufingerstraße 24, 80331 München, Germany

www.ingramcontent.com/pod-product-compliance
Lightning Source LLC
Chambersburg PA
CBHW051752230426
43670CB00012B/2259